Reconstructing Eden

Reconstructing Eden

Achieving Your Inner Paradise

Joyce Fern Glasser, Ph.D.

iUniverse, Inc.
New York Lincoln Shanghai

Reconstructing Eden
Achieving Your Inner Paradise

iUniverse books may be ordered through booksellers or by contacting:

iUniverse
2021 Pine Lake Road, Suite 100
Lincoln, NE 68512
www.iuniverse.com
1-800-Authors (1-800-288-4677)

ISBN-13: 978-0-595-37357-4 (pbk)
ISBN-13: 978-0-595-81754-2 (ebk)
ISBN-10: 0-595-37357-7 (pbk)
ISBN-10: 0-595-81754-8 (ebk)

Printed in the United States of America

Contents

About the Author

At the age of ten, the author's father led his little girl to believe she would write the greatest book ever written. As she learned in high school and college, her writing, while readable, does not elevate her to such status. Her goal then became to meet this belief her father instilled by writing about something great. That something great is the gleaned understandings from using what <u>is</u> her gift—that of being a healer/teacher. <u>Reconstructing Eden, Achieving Your Inner Paradise</u> shares what may be classified as revolutionary, the reconstruction of the negative aspects of personality in a matter of hours—not years.

Speaking of years, in these, the author's senior years—age sixty-seven to be exact, living each moment, living in the precious now, seems paramount. Rather than seeking out a ghost writer, Dr. Glasser chose to write this book on her own and self publish it first. It is then her intent to seek a publisher with a skilled writer on staff to sophisticate this presentation. Be that as it may, at least for the present, the basics of the personality reconstruction process have been preserved here.

Dr. Glasser became a psychotherapist as a mid-life career change. At age thirty-nine, she went back to school to study educational and clinical psychology. The driving force was seeking the kind of education that would help her ease pain and suffering in the world. Her Ph.D. in hand, she became licensed to practice as

a Mental Health Counselor in the State of Florida in 1982. As a result of fortu-
itous circumstances soon thereafter, she became awed with a psychotherapeutic
tool called hypnosis. Moreover, she experienced a profound spiritual miracle that
has incredibly potentiated her work. This book reflects the richness of Dr.
Glasser's blessings and the results of psychotherapeutically sharing them over the
past two decades.

Besides further book writing, it is Dr. Glasser's primary goal to apprentice
mental health professionals in Systematic Neuro Linguistic Reprogramming otherwise referred to here as "Core Healing". (She would like to see Core Healing
Centers in every neighborhood in the world.) Another goal is to lecture wherever
invited as well as to teach graduate level courses at a University. Dr. Glasser wel-
comes you to her web site at drjoyceglasser.com.

In Loving Memory

Sylvia Glasser, My mother

Daniel D. Glasser, My Father

With Everlasting Gratitude

Joyce Ann Morris

Donald Tyrell

Pamela Hutul Ross

Madelaine Frishman

Shirley Ellen Anderson

An Onymous

With Humble Admiration

Gautama Siddhartha

Mohatma Gandi

The Reverend Martin Luther King Junior

Oprah Winfrey

With Special Love

Mary Glasser Paladino

Emily Glasser Susman

Daniel Robert Glasser

Introduction

Why? Why do we behave as we do? Why do differences of behavior occur from one individual to another? Unless there is some anomaly, why do we all have two eyes, ten toes, two arms, two legs, etcetera, yet we do not all act alike? Why? Why do some of us seem relatively serene and most of us not? And why has it seemed that our personalities are relatively immutable? The catch all explanation is often, "it must be genetic".

But, what if so much ascribed to being genetic isn't? What then, beyond sociological factors, could explain why hordes of people are obese? (See Addendum II.) Why do so many people find it so difficult to quit smoking? Why do so many get drunk routinely? Why do people have difficulty with public speaking? Why do people complain of low self-esteem? Why do people create imaginary enemies? How does an anxiety disorder develop? How does depression happen? Why do people do horrible things? Why is suicide the ninth leading cause of death in our country? Why do people blame either God or the devil when terrible things happen?

Actually, and primarily, our troubles stem from faulty thinking called a thought disorder. Thought disorders take the form of negative self concepts and beliefs **that lead to** emotional, physical, behavioral, relationship, and/or Spiritual problems. The Diagnostic and Statistical Manual of Mental Disorders IV needs updating. This professionals' guide needs to reflect the forgoing statement. Perhaps the Cognitive therapists have already arrived at that conclusion. Regardless, there should not be two basic categories of disorders Mood and Thought. All disorders, including those of mood, stem from negative thoughts about self, others, our institutions, our country, our world. Negative thoughts, I conjecture, can even change our DNA and create the appearance that Bi-Polar Disorder is genetic. I call it the disease of extreme perfectionism. (Read Dr. Ernest Rossi's book The Psychobiology of Mind Body Healing Using Hypnosis. (1986).)

You will find more thorough answers to the problems common to us as human beings here in this book. Additionally, this book explains how a professional can transition you out of your problems into a better way of being.

Reconstructing Eden, Achieving Your Inner Paradise, is based upon nineteen years of hundreds of success stories and, yes failure experiences too, and what has been learned from them. Moreover, Chapter 4 explains the method with which to achieve success by altering the unseemly aspects of personality.

Journey with me as this saga unfolds starting in Chapter 1. It all begins, with of all things, the story of Adam and Eve.

Chapter 1

Reconstructing Eden

Paradise, the Eden before temptation, conjures images of sublime grace. No fears, no angers just Adam, a man, Eve, a woman and nature all harmoniously co-existing. This Adam and Eve experience no dark knowledge. Why not leave well enough alone?

Why, John Dunne asked so many hundreds of years ago, was <u>Paradise Lost</u>? Why, did an all powerful God allow a lesser being, a fallen angel, tempt Eve to bite from the fruit filled tree that would provide knowledge about good and evil? Dunne's answer? There is no real virtue without *choice*, the choice to choose between good and evil. God has thus allowed the creation of meaningful life, a life of potential virtue, virtue achieved not Vestal Virgins' defended.

Another view! Upright beings emerge from the original Eve, a dark woman of Africa. Depending on migratory direction, pigmentation for northern sojourners adjusts and lightens over the millennia in response to the sun's light and it's effects on body chemistry. Nostrils, flared to capture the dense Equatorial air, narrow restricting frigid air. Our ancestors multiply. Regional languages develop.

Migratory, whenever survival dictated, tribes would roam and some would be the explorers of vast expanses. The vast expanses kept shrinking in their ability to feed as the numbers of beings eventually began to outpace their environment to support them. Waste matter threatens, the planet rapaciously plucked weakens.

Are our origins evolutionary versus Senescent Being originated? Actually, truth be told, the answer may be that both are in their way correct. It's not about religion, it is about truth. The study of physics may yet prove the latter. As theories they are presentable. At this time, the former simply seems more defensible.

No matter the exact lineage, what is clear now is that humans have choice. Some are free to exhibit virtue. They make loving choices. Others, defile their soul within the confines of foul conviction. How does this divergency happen?

Why doesn't God rescue us from an omnipresent rampage on civilized living? Why, when in dire predicament, we beseech the Almighty, and no help seems to come? Why are we seemingly abandoned in our plight? Or, is there help we don't recognize as such, a type that does not infantilize?

One scary and anger provoking conclusion! We must not be worthy of salvation. We must only be worthy of far worse than the hell we are creating for ourselves. And thus, there are internal cries of desperation and self abdication.

Fear, ugly fear! It can get magnified and multiplied with efforts for self-preservation and, at times, that attendant desperation. Hell and damnation can seem real. Quivering and helpless seeming, we become ripe to be duped and misled for venial, self-serving purpose. Just act authoritatively, confidently and righteously and we can become the obedient…to the wrong gods.

God, when using Dunne's interpretation of the fall from grace, can be construed as having faith in us rather than simply being angry at Adam and Eve. Rather than viewing heedlessness of God's advice as the original sin, we need to capture that faith in ourselves and in God's purpose for <u>allowing</u> human choice. Certainly, with choice, there is consequent human error. Nonetheless, I thank God for honoring us as the senescent beings that we are.

While we have choices that can lead to harm, we are also capable of exercising choices inherently loving, basically beneficial for self and others, choices that are nourishing of life and of the God within you and me and within all living things. I choose to learn from my mistakes, and yours, and thus to become wiser. I choose to make myself readily available to, as well as nurture, the Holy Spirit that is within me. I choose to learn from the great teachers through whose teachings I can better embrace all others with compassion. But my view of God has to allow me that opportunity. I cannot succumb to being a mindless follower taught to quake if I am not *heedful* of the "inspired" and absolute purported word of an often frighteningly described God.

God, in the Biblical Adam and Eve story, was depicted as the punitive parent. Which God do we choose? Do we choose God the wrathful, the

God of Noah, the God of Job, the jealous God, the abandoning God of Revelation, *or* a God who does not trash people, punish them or heap agony upon a person simply to make a point? These conflicted, ugly models of the Almighty are played out in representational manner in families around the world. There are wrathful parents. There are punitive parents. There are punishing and unrelentingly demanding parents. There are autocratic father-mothers. These models of 'family' life lead to war, mindless followers, more such ugly parenting as well as hatefulness with all it's attendant terrible consequences.

Where there are fear and anger fomenting, real Godliness shrivels. On the other hand, where parents exemplify compassion, self-discipline, respectfulness, kindness and forgiveness, Godliness swells. Moreover, parental loving kindness leads to neighborliness. My mission, and I would hope yours, is to be the ambassador of the latter godly parenting/leadership model. Let us, therefore, reconstruct paradise within ourselves. Then we will be free to parent our children lovingly, and, our earth as well. In so far as we are able, our mission must be to <u>reconstruct</u> the often damaged Eden within and around us. My conviction is that **only** <u>by taking respon-sibility, by handling blame and fault with dignity, and thereby learning from our mistakes</u> can we *earn* and <u>truly savor</u> paradise. This reconstruction commitment will bear the fruit of true and lasting peace.

In God's grace resides our salvation. Quality life resides in our willingness and our freedom to assume full responsibility for ourselves and our conduct. It is unseemly for an adult to do any less. Top that with our allegiance to peace, achievable by each one of us <u>Reconstructing Eden</u>, just imagine what a joyous type of existence becomes possible even in this less than perfect world. It is our only way, in human form, to revel in this the Eden with which God has so lavishly gifted us. Let us sweep ourselves clean of fear and of anger based conviction. Let us exemplify loving kindness and not allow ourselves to be duped by venial purpose.

This book teaches how we can at last succeed, how we can augment peace one by one of us. The technology is available to reconstruct the negative aspects of ourselves by altering our personalities once thought immutable. In gifting ourselves with enlightenment, with the freedom to love, to live and let live, to absent domination, to relinquish enslavement to our fears, and eschew ugly, hurtful anger, we will then provide enviable legacy.

<u>Reconstructing Eden</u> requires responsible stewardship. By each of us pledging our beings as a trustee of peace, by each of us emptying our internal worlds of unremitting strife, by coming to know God in Truth as Unconditionally Loving, then we will be abundantly ready to reconstruct our earthly paradise.

Join the choir, be a trustee, become an ambassador of peace. Know the reward of self reconstruction. Serenity is incredibly sweet. Your happiness, I believe, is God's purpose for you. It is only then, that as a result of your happiness and serenity will your children be vessels of such emulation. Gift yourself, gift your children. Earn it for yourself and them with a new allegiance. Eschew the gods of righteousness, sin and damnation, those of arrogant absolutism and terrorism, those who cultivate a fear of God and enslavement to mindless conviction. Align with those of humble, and loving style, a style free of guile.

Chapter 2

The Minds and How They Work

The brain, the gray matter housed within our skulls, facilitates sensory reception, interpretation, and, response. How well it functions depends on genetics, whether it is injured or not, whether it is actively stimulated for growth of functioning, whether it is properly fed systemically speaking, and, how, regionally over time, it may have become altered. As I paint these broad strokes of explanation, remember, I am not a brain specialist. That is the expertise of neurologists. Be that as it may, even in rudimentary fashion, this explanation hopefully does well enough to create a distinction between the brain's functions and how the mind works.

The mind's functioning is facilitated in various locations or parts of the brain. The neurotransmitters known as hormones play their part as well. While the mind and it's functioning can be effected by the brain's relative healthfulness and efficiency, conversely, the mind can affect the quality of brain function.

Regarding how the brain can affect the mind, here is one example. Mental retardation, due to genetics or to injury, can logically affect how swiftly data is accessed and sorted as well as the quality of the storage facility from which that individual can draw for appropriate response.

An example of how the mind can affect the brain's functioning is when an accumulation of negative self concepts and beliefs frequently lead a person to feeling out of control. Unremedied out of control struggles can lead to feelings of despair. Feelings of despair can lead to the depression of serotonin levels which then exacerbate feelings of depression. Serotonin, a hormone, is called the feel good chemical of the brain.

The mind has two parts, the conscious and the subconscious. These two parts of the mind make up the whole and serve different functions. Yet, the conscious and the subconscious work together as a unit. The conscious part funnels information via our various sensory channels to the subconscious. The conscious part makes judgements. It evaluates. It makes decisions based on the evaluation(s). However, the subconscious part is the boss.

The conscious part of the mind, generally, is not aware of what is going on with it's partner, the subconscious. Interestingly, however, the subconscious is always aware of what is going on with the conscious mind.

The subconscious mind is the part responsible for an individual's response based on the information channeled through the various sensory channels, i.e., sight, sound, smell, taste, and, the feel of something. When the conscious mind evaluates, then makes a decision based upon the information received, the subconscious either allows that decision to proceed or not based upon that individual's accumulated self concepts and beliefs. If a person makes a decision to lose weight, for example, an intra-psychic battle may ensue. Implementation becomes stymied. Why? Because the decision of the conscious is not in harmony with the subconscious. On the other hand, when a decision is consciously derived and that decision is in harmony with the subconscious, that person will be able to actualize the decision *effortlessly*. The goal of psychotherapy is to be of one mind where the conscious and subconscious are in harmony as your best self. Serenity and self confidence ensue. (See Chapter 5 for ideas on being that best self.)

My colleagues and I agree on the name of that part of the mind called the conscious. Most disagree with me regarding the name of the other. It is an extremely important disagreement that at first may seem trivial. I call the other part of the mind the subconscious and they the unconscious. It is a significant distinction based on the simple but yet profoundly different meanings of these two prefixes. Sub means below or under. Un means not. The importance of this distinction leads to a clear understanding, or, less than accurate understanding of the mind's functioning. If one does not clearly comprehend a particular mind's function, a psychotherapist is assuredly hampered in relative healing effectiveness.

If what is being said with the use of the word unconscious that a person is not always consciously aware of their thoughts, that would be true. A cognition can flit by so quickly, that a person's conscious mind, not attuned, not disciplined, and rather sluggish by comparison, misses that thought and often quite completely. If it is said that we are not fully aware of why we act and feel the way we do in any given moment that would also be true. Generally, however, when we say a person is unconscious, it suggests that person is 'out cold'. The individual is there in body *but* neither mind is available.

To remove ambiguity, I relegate the meaning of unconscious to the medical domain as in knocked out cold or those times when both minds are asleep at night as a part of the brain's normal functioning. It is a physician's job to deal with an injury to the brain and physiologically induced sleep malfunction. An example of the former! The back of a man's head receives blunt force trauma. He is rendered <u>un</u>conscious and then is robbed. The injury to his brain may be minor or significant. He may have a concussion, tissue damage, etc. A brain specialist may be needed to treat these injuries. It is not a mind repair problem, at least, not initially.

It would be a reasonable assumption that the traumatic event may result in a different kind of damage to the individual, a non-physiological one. He may develop a post traumatic stress reaction. It is then that *a mind doctor* would be called upon *to repair the negative behavioral and/or emotional effects* from the incident. And, that repair must be done in both domains, the conscious and the subconscious. It is the subconscious that produces nightmarish flashbacks. In this case, the flashbacks are those that are relevant to walking on that particular street near his home where the incident happened and the momentary awareness of being attacked before passing out. It is the conscious mind that needs to funnel information to the subconscious to help with understanding the effects of the trauma and what ameliorative steps need to be taken. The beliefs, at the subconscious level, will either actualize what was learned or stymie what needs doing. A helpful belief would be: "it is okay to get help from a mental health professional". A detracting belief would be: "I'm a fix it yourself kind of guy."

If I were to call the subconscious "the unconscious" there is the presumption, by definition, of unavailability of that mind and worse the unavailability of the wealth of knowledge catalogued in the subconscious. Therefore, the big deal about *sub* or *un* is, **sub** <u>implies that information is there to be found. It is just *below* the surface of conscious awareness.</u> All we need then is a good submarine herein called a process with which to submerge and retrieve the data. The data, in the form of negative self concepts and beliefs plus imprinted traumatic memories and attendant feelings, if less than severe, needs to be brought to the surface in order to resolve people's problems whether the problems be behavioral, emotional, relational, physical, and/or Spiritual.

"Seek the truth, it sets you free." Knowledge, in the form of truth, is power. <u>A problem can not be solved without the knowledge of the truths behind the problem.</u> People think they know why they do what they do. If they truly did know the *all* of why their problems existed, they would not have the problems. A problem can not be completely resolved without the whole truth. Profoundly, therefore, seeking the truth for the sake of freedom from one's problems emphasizes the big deal between sub and un. <u>Where</u> can you find the truth if the presumption is that a person is <u>*not*</u> consciously aware of what they need to know to solve a particular problem? The truth is certainly not in the psychotherapist.

The psychotherapist has been trained to be the one who must be posited with the truth of the matter and then to adjust the client's thinking according to that truth. Moreover, the professional then chooses whatever psychotherapeutic remedy is deemed appropriate to transition the client to a better place based on those assumed truths. The only way I know to make a mistake is by an incorrect assumption.

The assumed truths are then treated, quite usually, with Cognitive Therapy. Some psychotherapists are pretty good at what boils down to educated guess work based on training, intuitive ability, and, professional experience so some amelioration may happen for a client. However, can you really and quite thoroughly fix something and yet at the same time be ignorant of what actually needs fixing? Can you free the individual of their misery without knowing the truths that can be uniquely theirs that are creating the problem? Of course not!

Sadly, and, quite usually, psychotherapists are trained into limited know how. They have not been taught the value of the <u>sub</u>conscious. They do not know how to access the wealth within the subconscious because until now, it seems that the information has not been available to teach. Apparently, it has not been known how to deal fortuitously with the subconscious.

Psychotherapists are all too often trained in just 'talk therapy'. Talk therapy primarily engages the conscious mind which is a peanut of awareness by comparison to the subconscious mind. An example! How aware of the world were you at the age of five? Not very! How aware of the world are you now? Considerably more aware. This vastly greater awareness mind is the <u>sub</u>conscious.

"Core healing", a phrase used by many of my clients to describe the effects of the process experienced, engages both minds. The conscious mind identifies the problems that it has judged to be problematic. The conscious mind of a client is educated by the "core healing" therapist as to the understandings necessary for that person to cooperate. The conscious mind funnels information to the subconscious. The conscious mind is essential during a "core healing" session for it facilitates conversation. Through the use of hypnosis, the subconscious is additionally accessed. I call it "working with the whole enchilada". <u>Both minds are positioned to work together for common cause</u>, the resolution of the problems presented by the client for therapy.

Hypnosis is the gentlest way to open the door to the wealth of truth and the wealth of awareness catalogued in the subconscious mind. Therefore, without hypnosis, the degree of healing effect can be extremely limited. Fortunately, more and more psychotherapists are learning about hypnosis and some colleges are beginning to train future therapists in it's use.

<u>All truth of why a person does what they do exists at the **sub**conscious level</u>. Since it is available, why guess? Why not go to the source? Why aren't we training psychotherapists to do that? <u>Such training is not typically provided because this phenomenon is not generally known.</u> No professionals that I know got lucky the way I did and experienced therapy using hypnosis with Gerald Kein or one of his proteges. What I deducted from that

therapeutic experience is the essentialness of hypnosis, <u>especially, the way it was used</u>. <u>It was a hypnotherapeutic process</u> that facilitated the easy change of my behavior in terms of a long standing problem. I have built upon that seminal learning/healing experience and what you will find in Chapter 4 is a description of that broadened process <u>as well as</u> <u>the important knowledge gleaned </u>from decades of it's use.

Hypnosis opens the door to <u>the subconscious mind, the storehouse</u> <u>of the thousands of self concepts and beliefs both positive and negative</u> <u>that in sum define an individual's personality. The subconscious con-</u> <u>trols the **all** of a person's functioning</u>. I learned these basics not during my doctoral studies but by deduction from my experience with a student of Mr. Kein's by the name of Kathy Angelli. She brought my subconscious into harmony with the wish of my conscious mind to eat with control. I was stunned. How did such improved control occur so quickly? Why, after but one session, did the control remain? How could the compulsiveness just evaporate when I was struggling with this problem most of my life? Needless to say, I became a believer as well as an avid learner about using the tool called hypnosis.

Hypnosis, as mentioned earlier, provides access to the subconscious. Not only is the subconscious a vast warehouse of data accumulated by an individual, but it<u> is also a vast computer network charged with the job of</u> <u>data processor.</u> The subconscious causes a person to react to sensory input (stimuli) <u>in automated, at the speed of light, type fashion</u>. The response, in behavioral terms, is based upon an individual's self concepts and beliefs both positive and negative.

The subconscious is a vast library housing this catalogued data of negative and positive self concepts and beliefs along with the emotional content associated with the retained seminal memories. Instantaneously, the data, relevant to the stimulus, is retrieved from the current catalogue or from the archives. (A contrived way of describing this phenomenon is with the concept of chakras.) The assortment retrieved is based upon the stimulus and produces a logical, though not necessarily desirable, behavioral and/or emotional and/or physiological response.

The subconscious mind is an amoral entity meaning it makes no value judgements. It just reacts based on the constellation of beliefs that are relevant. Telling a recalcitrant person the logic of a better behavior is generally a waste of breath, unless, luckily you hit on a rationalle that connects with a positive self concept or belief that then allows that person compliance with a positive suggestion. In other words, receiving advice, regardless of source, may have minimal, if any, positive outcome depending upon a person's self concepts and beliefs. So a mother, a father, a minister, a rabbi, a teacher, a counselor, a self-help book, may be rendered useless in their attempt to salvage an individual from self destructive behavior. <u>The assumption that people have free will to do what is logically right or is in their best interests is faulty.</u> **<u>People can only do what their assortment of self concepts and beliefs allow.</u>** They may exercise the power of positive thinking and/or action **only** when their assortment of positives promote such positive response, <u>and</u>, when their negatives do not interfere.

The job of the conscious mind, as mentioned earlier, is to make judgements. How well it evaluates, how good the judgements are, depends upon the quality of an individual's education. The education retained becomes some of that person's self concepts and beliefs. (See Chapter 3 for an in depth explanation about how this accumulation of self concept data occurs within the subconscious.)

The conscious mind can be viewed as the tip of the iceberg. The subconscious is the rest. It is that massive part that is below the surface. There are many systematic ways of reaching through the conscious mind to access the subconscious. Voice activated hypnosis, while it is not the only method of induction, is simply my method of choice. My voice acts like the sonar that locates the subconscious. My voice is my instrument. It funnels through the conscious mind to the subconscious. But more than that, hypnosis alters the brain wave patterns that afford the energy with which to open the flap to enter the teepee of the full dimension of the mind. And, of no small additional benefit, this tapped energy source can enhance with radiance the Spiritual domain especially so when the negativity residing at the subconscious level is deleted and replaced with positivity.

(There are certain religious groups that will not allow their membership to partake of hypnosis. It seems like a fight for the control of a person's mind. That may be their goal, but it cannot be the goal of psychotherapy. The goal of psychotherapy has to be to enhance the client's <u>self</u> control because we become morally defunct when <u>other</u> controlled. Waco, Texas comes to mind as an example.)

Finding the truths regarding why a problem exists allows the potential of leaving that problem behind. In trance, while hypnotized, this truth-seeking journey about the origins of a person's problems is enhanced significantly. Once truths are uncovered (utilizing such hypnotherapeutic techniques as age regression, if no severe trauma history is present, as well as ideo-motor signaling), there are a wonderful array of psychotherapeutic techniques (such as Cognitive, Reality, and, Behavioral, plus Transactional Analysis and Inner Child work) with which "core healing" can be achieved. (See Chapter 4 for the goals of "core healing".) To be most effective, let me reiterate, <u>comprehensive healing work</u> must occur in the domain of the subconscious, which <u>requires hypnosis</u>.

During a hypnotherapeutic session, the job of the conscious mind is to be a facilitator of speech, funnel suggestions to the subconscious, and, be an auditory witness. It is cautiously, that the evaluative function of the conscious mind is engaged. If too much of it's critical faculty is relied upon, unwittingly, the person can be removed from the hypnotic state. The consequence of that would be the prohibiting of constructive change in the subconscious (the computer mind).

In the domain of the subconscious, each of us can have similar, even the same and yet some very unique beliefs that react to the constant bombardment of everyday and not so everyday stimuli. Therefore, at times, we can behave and/or feel similarly, the same or quite differently.

When a person's sensory organs transmit the reception of a sound, a smell, a touch, a visual image, a taste, or any combination of these to the subconscious mind, <u>instantaneously</u>, the subconscious mind orchestrates a behavioral and/or an emotional and/or a physiological response based on the relevant, assorted beliefs a person holds. I call that assortment a constellation. As mentioned earlier, the response may or may not be appropriate, may or may not be constructive, may or may not be honest, etc. The mechanistic, amoral, non-evaluative, response is activated by the stimulus. Quite simply, the relevant constellation of beliefs are called into play and produce a logical, though not necessarily desirable, response. Therefore, reasoning with a person might 'fall on deaf ears'. The conscious mind, which is the evaluative mind, may agree, for example, that doing homework is a good idea. However, if one's self concept is that of stupid, and/or lazy, and/or failure, and/or loser, that person cannot possibly implement in any studious fashion, the wise suggestion to do homework. The negative self concepts over-ride any fantasy that youngster may have to be an astronaut, for example. Consequently, no homework gets done, no learning achieved, no ambition, no dream potentiated.

For healthy change to take place, the negative self concepts and beliefs that are generating a particular problem, not only have to be identified but also **deleted** **and then** <u>replaced with positive opposites</u>. To reiterate, all these steps must take place in the domain of the subconscious, the computer center. (These steps are explained in Chapter 4.)

The subconscious mind governs the everything of a person. The conscious mind is not in control, it is not 'the captain of the ship'. So to say to a person when they behave badly, "you should have known better", is unfair. It is wishful thinking and in a sense irrelevant because of the fact that the beliefs at the subconscious level control response. **An 'appropriate' choice, a 'wise' decision can only be made if there are positive self concepts and beliefs available with no or minimal competing negatives with which to arrive at such good conclusion.** As the apt expression goes, 'you can't make a silk purse out of a sow's ear'. You can not expect a person riddled with predominantly negative self concepts and beliefs to necessarily 'do the right thing'.

In order to have good conclusion, it must be realized that no individual can be blamed for the predicament of their exhibiting bad or evil conduct. Moreover, we cannot blame the devil. The devil does not exist. The devil is simply a horribly unfortunate, archaic metaphor to explain why people do the bad, hurtful and even evil things they sometimes do. While individuals cannot be blamed for poor conduct choices, nonetheless, they must be asked to take responsibility for correcting bad conduct. Sadly, however, their belief systems may not even permit them that.

We have until now, quite ignorantly, been perpetuating negative history within ourselves, our families, our communities, our religious institutions, our country, and, our world. That is why this book is being written. The understandings presented in this book, when mobilized broadly, can stop negative history from repeating itself. We can wage civilized war on the evil conduct that seems to relentlessly move our world toward what seems to be the ultimate destruction of our Eden.

It is imperative that such destructive myths as the devil and original sin be relegated to oblivion because they themselves become negative self concepts and beliefs that perpetuate a negative momentum. It was so sad to hear a father explain his child's misguided, addicted, and, illegal behavior in the only way he knew to conclude…as being of the devil possessed. What horribly perpetuated and misguided nonsense. I feel sorry for him and, most especially, his child, and us. **If the subconscious of that young-ster accepts that belief as truth, it will enact that belief.** Consequently, that young person will then behave based on past exposure to the concept and the definitions absorbed subconsciously. In whatever ways that young person interprets "by the devil possessed"will now become behavior actu-alized. And so the mess that young person is in becomes exacerbated. However, the father has just relieved himself and his wife of the responsi-bility. A somber drum roll please…. it became the devil's fault. Similarly, I recently read of a young man in his early twenties engaging in vigorous exercise. He went into cardiac arrest. An autopsy was done. At three hun-dred pounds was it any wonder that the fellow had an enlarged heart and bad coronary arteries? His parent's response to the tragedy? Another somber drum roll please…..''We don't understand why the Lord took him because he was such a decent man".

As human beings, the folks alluded to above are still reaching for understandings for why bad things happen. In the instances in the forgoing paragraph, the excuses were culled from religious mythology. Pardon me if I sounded irreverent in the former paragraph but I have witnessed more and more parents absenting themselves from responsibility for their children's unfortunate outcomes since 1960, after my first year as a fourth grade teacher. (Becoming a psychotherapist was a mid life career change for me.)

That parents are not helped to examine themselves for cause effect relationship perpetuates such tragedies. Would it not be a breath of fresh air for the parents of the young fellow who collapsed to acknowledge that they should not have rewarded their child with food, and/or that they taught him to enjoy starches, and/or that they gave him a nickname celebrating being porky, and/or because he was a guy, that it was okay for him to be really big, like a linebacker, etcetera. Would it not be great for such folks to meet with other folks compassionately sharing their failures and beseeching other parents not to make the mistakes they did? Wow, I would stand up and cheer. This book is my best attempt at teaching what seems to me to be the most important of ways to reconstruct ourselves to make such openness, such responsibility taking happen. Without an adjustment in the collective mind that is us, negative history will continue to repeat itself. More obese people will collapse and die unnecessarily.

I pray that armed with the information provided in this book, we will at last prevent a fear of being at fault. As children, punitive, loud, harshly accusing type of parenting causes us to learn to recoil at the notion of being at fault. We must pause and refuse to run from our sometimes horrible mistakes. We must accept, reflect and reconstruct our ways in order to keep negative history from repeating itself. By admitting that to some degree or other we are <u>all</u> faulty, and then committing ourselves to shaping up, then there is real hope for the future.

It is only through embracing responsibility, wholesome education, and, through the funnel of the conscious into the subconscious, that we can begin the systematic task of liberating ourselves from the misery of being 'blind sighted'. We have to dedicate ourselves to unlearning fear based lessons, learning love based ones instead as well as engaging ourselves in this rather amazingly brief task of <u>Reconstructing Eden</u>. And, the key to this Kingdom is the tool called hypnosis.(In ten and a half to fourteen hours of work, this reconstruction for so many of us can be accomplished quickly.)

As an aside, when you read <u>The Gnostic Gospels</u> by Elaine Pagels, notice two things. One, the word "trance" is frequently used as a way to come to know our benevolent God. Trance is another word for hypnosis. Two, the tenor of these Gospels seems different than <u>The New Testament</u> gospels. <u>The Gnostic Gospels</u> do not strike me as being frightening as in the <u>intent</u> to frighten. They seem more to be in just celebratory fashion reporting the good news.

Chapter 3

How We Become Who We Are

A sperm penetrates an ovum. Conception occurs. Is a person then coded the self concept Buddhist because the parents are? No, of course not. That identity is nurtured. Is a person coded genetically to steal? No, there is no such genetic defect called "thief". Tougher questions! An infant tends to be skittish, agitated and has an easy startle reaction. Is that infant wired with an anxiety disorder? What is sometimes referred to as the "old brain", the prehistoric part of the brain that facilitates the fright/fright response, is it malfunctioning and thus resulting in hyper vigilance and sensitivity? Maybe! Or, as in the case of some of my clients, they were anxiety sensitized while developing in the uterus of their birth mothers. Mothers' and even dads' mood states and behaviors affect the fetus.

During gestation, a child's personality begins to develop based upon the relevant degree of hospitableness of the environment. Obstetricians are advising pregnant parents to talk lovingly to their unborn child and to play classical music with an earphone to the belly of the pregnant mom. At least some of what was thought to be genetic (one's inborn "nature") is moving over to the other column called "nurture". Parents are encouraged to create an environment, for example, that *nurtures* the mathematical ability of the developing fetus by playing Mozart.

Six weeks into gestation, the brain is formed. It's neural network is in a state of rapid growth and expansion. With this network in place, the fetus is ready to 'pick up vibes', an excellent expression to fit this context. Obviously, in utero, the fetus has no language to translate felt senses into words. But 'feeling' data of consequence is imprinted into the subconscious. After birth, when language develops, words are then available to describe the experience. These words become concepts and/or beliefs about oneself, and, like all self concepts they are housed and catalogued in the subconscious. As yet, I have not met anyone who was consciously aware of in utero experience. Under hypnosis, with access to the subconscious, I have.

What are the beliefs a fetus might typically develop. They are: "I am wanted", "I'm lovable". These types of feelings create survival security. Conversely, "I am not wanted, I shouldn't exist"; "I'm anxious"; "I'm sad"; "I must be no good" and/or "not good enough"; "I'm scared to come into and be in the world"; "I deserve to be abandoned"; "I must be ugly"; these feelings create at minimum insecurity. Maximally, the negative reflections can generate being terrified to come into the world. Moreover, a physiological response such as breach birth or a lowered and blocking placenta would seem likely. Preposterous? Not according to my experience. The subconscious governs one's physiology.

Keep in mind when I am working with a person, I am working through their problems. Therefore, I am in search of the negatives that have created the problems. The foregoing negatives, I have witnessed and experienced with my clients. As to the positives, I conjecture their existence based upon ease of delivery and a happy, gurgling little one that is placed in a mother's arms. There is no bad seed. There are only bad seminal experiences. For example, an adopted new born usually has been imprinted by virtue of the birth parents 'rejecting' the child with a host of negative vibes about themselves that make them behave in ways very difficult for the adopted parents to handle. Based on such understandings as presented in this book, a child management program could be developed and required of parents approved for adoption.

Another example of a bad seminal event is this one. While hypnotized, a client relived a trauma related to his presenting problem of not being able to quit smoking. He was aware consciously that he did not care particularly whether he lived or died. Using a technique called hypnotic age regression, this client was regressed to the most critical, the most relevant memory related to this issue. The memory that came up was from when he was a fetus. He relived feeling himself in suspension. He became aware that his mother was agitated. She had just told her husband, his father, that she was pregnant. The father became enraged, and said, "how dare you to have become pregnant". A very sad, perverse and laughable comment until in the next instant he savagely kicked his wife's belly. Even though suspended in and protected by the amniotic fluid, my client felt the turbulence. When asked how he was feeling during this relived experience, it was already obvious he felt terrified. He additionally reported feeling like he shouldn't exist. In the presence of such trauma, this ugly memory itself imprinted into the subconscious. Moreover, <u>the attendant negative feelings</u> themselves <u>become</u> such <u>negative self concepts</u> as: "I am a person who is terrified of those upon whom I am dependent"; and, "I am a person who should not exist". (See Chapter 4 for a discussion regarding the issue of the thorough reconstructive healing work necessary for the negative effects of such trauma. None of us are trauma free.)

This seminal event and attendant feelings produced the additional self concepts nervous, unworthy, not good enough, etc. Smokers generally have much discomfort with the negative feelings derived from these types of self concepts. Then, by observation of other smokers, their subconscious absorbs the belief that such uneasiness, such discomfort can be managed with the cigarette. Though not in fact true, because nicotine as a drug is not a relaxant but a stimulant, the ever so pervasively powerful subconscious can adjust the body's chemistry to make relaxation the effect of inhaling a stimulant. Additionally, the act of taking a break in order to smoke is what is in fact relaxing even if it's only the relatively brief distraction of the time it takes to light up and take the first puff.

Until negative seminal events are rectified at the subconscious level, and the resulting negative self concepts and beliefs deleted and replaced with positives, then, and only then, can an inveterate smoker become a non smoker. If in addition to becoming a non smoker, a smoker wanted to assume the personality of a non smoker, positive self concepts such as optimist, out going, forgiving of self, and easy going would facilitate that goal.

Compounding the problem of a smoker becoming a non smoker is that generally most youngsters are raised by methods of external control as opposed to self control. Therefore, the control for discomforting feelings causes a person to reach <u>outside</u> oneself for that control and in this case they <u>learn</u> to turn to the cigarette.

<u>People have learned to posit the acquisition of temporary feelings of control from initial, and seemingly positive, effects from drugs, alcohol, food, nicotine, sex, gambling, anger, auditory halucinations, competitive conduct regardless of costs, etc.</u> Once the use of a substance or activity gives any seemingly positive support in managing a problem, the belief is established that using that substance or engaging in that activity in the manner when first engaged is a good idea. They may also suffer the belief that if some is good, more must be better. Stepping back from such maladaptive coping modes then becomes difficult until these reinforcing beliefs are changed as well as the belief regarding the usefulness of a particular mode or modes.

Managing feelings of anger, emptiness, defenselessness, relentless intensity, literal hunger pangs (because of a fear of gaining weight) are often accomplished seemingly when sucking down, pushing down any or all of these feelings with smoke. By smoking, they have come to believe they can better keep their anger in check, their weight down, take breaks, keep others at bay, and, fill the void. (As it is believed, so shall it be or so shall it seem.)

When a person quits smoking 'cold turkey' and 'it was a cake walk' for them, it is because any negative self concepts were minimally contributive to the problem and their positives were supportive of quitting. My work with hundreds of smokers strongly suggests that <u>nicotine, while toxic, is **not** addictive</u>. Rather, the unfortunate constellation of negative self concepts and beliefs in a milieu of <u>other</u> control creates the <u>dependency</u> issues and forces a person to smoke. No amount of logic to the contrary can foster the changes necessary without access to the subconscious.

By the way, we contribute to the negative constellation of self concepts by describing a smoker as *"diehard"* or "addicted". The definitions of these words compound the problem. Smokers who add the words diehard or addicted into their self descriptor lexicon must now <u>act</u> their definition of these words. Having the self concept "addict", quite likely, will convey the idea to the subconscious to make quitting a struggle. A diehard will die the hard way. *As you believe it so shall it be.*

<u>Negative labeling of a person as opposed to a behavior reduces that person's self esteem and their relative degree of self control. One by one, negative labels are absorbed. A person's potential for wholesome self direction is weakened if not destroyed.</u>

In conclusion, the man spoken about came into this world under terrifying, traumatic circumstance. As a result he developed a host of negative self concepts and beliefs. Collectively, this constellation would be identified as nervousness and self destructiveness. Observing others who were nervous and self destructive and how they managed such self concepts, he too learned and became a smoker.

I can only conjecture, based upon the millions of doses of psycho-tropic drugs prescribed to children, as well as their increasing rate of suicide, how many hundreds of thousands of youngsters came into the world with negative beginnings as well.

During infancy, a key negative self concept generated is a <u>fear of being alone, of being abandoned</u>. Parents cannot possibly be there for their infant '24/7'. Besides the natural needs of a human being for things like sleeping, going to the bathroom, and bathing plus the intrusions of circumstance, these all can call the parent away. The phone rings, a neighbor knocks at the door pleading for help with an emergency, another child needs attention, dad gets home and reports he lost his job to outsourcing, etcetera. At times, isn't it virtually impossible not to leave an infant alone and hopefully in the safety of the crib? If the infant becomes frightened or worse traumatized with feeling abandoned, the subconscious is accessed and the negative reactive decisions: "I must deserve to be abandoned" and/or "I am scared to be left alone" are developed. The cadre of one's beliefs accumulate.

(By the way, I would conjecture that the high rate of divorce, in significant part, is the result of that abandonment conviction. Consciously, most seem unaware that they have the belief that they 'deserve to be abandoned'. With that belief, people will pick fights with their spouse until the spouse leaves them. The subconscious creates the game plan based on the 'soft spots' of the spouse. Anger behavior is excellent for suffocating love.)

Now, imagine how a welcomed, happy infant will respond to the occasions of being left alone versus the child who feels unwanted, or ill timed or threatened in terms of it's very existence. So long as there is no trauma associated with having been left alone, such as a fire, the happy infant will be more inclined to feeling comfortable during the absence. The fear of being left alone will not be so likely, nor, if felt, not so intensely.

Negative self concepts, such as the negatives developed in utero as discussed earlier, will predispose an infant to a more intense response to being left alone. The fear of being left alone translates viscerally to a fear of dying. Quite literally, infants actually left alone, actually left unattended, are helpless beings that would in fact die with no one there to take care of them.

It is our nature to fear a threat to our life. That instinct is available at a very early age. Even from conception? I do not know. From birth forward, definitely, yes!

Most people grow up with some degree of fear of being alone. The highest intensity is literally being scared to death of such a predicament. Frequency of times being left alone, the duration each time, whether or not the infant's needs have been met just prior to the times of being left alone, a parent's reactions to the infant's crying while left alone such as with guilt and anger or soothingly, all such circumstances can exacerbate or alleviate the relative intensity of this fear. (A research question: Women, and even teens, do they get themselves pregnant driven by an intense fear of being alone? Is this factor, one among others, that together are mistakenly labeled as maternal instinct?)

<u>During childhood</u>, the process of self concept development and beliefs continues to compound. Over the course of a lifetime, we acquire thousands upon thousands if not millions of self concepts and beliefs both of positive and of negative nature and consequence. Self concepts accumulate by processes of observation ("I have the body of a girl".), by being labeled ("You are a good girl".), culturally ("I am of middle class background".), racially ("I am white".), reactively ("I learn from my mistakes".), religiously (ethics are important), etcetera.Over the years, some self concepts and beliefs are relinquished, and/or changed. Now, for example, "I am a woman". (The self concept girl is still there so at times you will hear senior citizens my age referring to their group as the "girls".)

During childhood, commonly acquired negative self concepts include "shy", "stupid", "unattractive", "fat", "bad", "loser"and "evil". Other critical negative self concepts that tend to get developed, if not already developed, are such self concepts as: "I'm not good enough"; "I'm unlovable"; "I don't deserve to be loved unconditionally"; and, "I must deserve to be abandoned".

The differences of a child's experiences in utero as well as after birth means that, contrary to popular misconception, children born into the same home are raised under different, even extremely different, circumstances. Their concepts of self are varied because moms and dads are not at the same places in their lives from one child to the next, not from a maturity, relationship, nor necessarily from an occupational or financial perspective. Moreover, one child already born presents an entirely different home environment for the second. The second born, in turn, creates a different environment, one that is frequently offensive to the dethroned first. Hence, sibling rivalry can erupt for what seems to them like limited parental attention. (Quite literally, a child can be scared to death not to have that attention.) Fighting ensues. The intensity and frequency of the fighting between the two children is dependent on the degree of the fear felt by either one or both of the children.

This reality of dissimilar circumstances can explain how the same home can provide different experiences that imprint different self concepts. These circumstances can create quite different children like a Cain and an Abel, for example.

Children's negative self concepts such as "I deserve to be abandoned" can get negatively reinforced through experiencing a father or a mother going off to war, or by the parents getting a divorce. Negative self concepts such as loser or dumb can be reinforced at school when not picked until last to be on a team, and, by frequently receiving negative academic feedback. Studies tend to confirm, that what is wrong is dwelled upon far more than what is right. Correcting does not, *ipso facto*, lead to correction. Moreover, additional negative self concepts can result when failures are more the menu of the day rather than successes. These negatives often include, "I'm not smart enough", "I can't do anything right", "I don't bother trying anymore".

Shyness, another negative self concept developed in childhood, is a significant contributing factor to nicotine, drug and alcohol dependency. Shyness is unwittingly developed in a child. As animal beings we are naturally <u>wary</u> of strangers and/or those bigger than us. Rather than complimenting a child for appropriate caution, a parent can often be heard to say to their child, "now, don't be shy". With even the smallest amount of fear felt, there is access to the subconscious mind. So, the child feeling some fear in the presence of what for them is a giant of a stranger, when that child is told they are "shy" that self concept is now imprinted into the subconscious. Until corrected subconsciously, that individual will feel shy as it was for them in the context of the situation when they were first labeled as such.

Shyness, as a self concept, produces discomforting feelings. Discomforting feelings agitate the individual to assuage that feeling. They may become reclusive, introverted, or when older a smoker using the cigarette for company. Shy folks may use alcohol or cannabis (pot) to reduce their inhibitions. They struggle between their fear of being alone, wanting real company and their shyness. It all depends on the degree of the shyness felt and the frequency and intensity of subsequent reinforcing events.

Another negative self concept most children develop, more so than the word dumb, is stupid. Name calling and shaming a child with this appellation are the general modes of inculcation. Have you ever heard an adult say something like, "I know I'm intelligent but there is a part of me that thinks of myself as stupid"?

It seems as if one of the biggest fears of just about everybody on the face of this earth is doing or saying something stupid. To admit to that fear, however, would be tantamount to acknowledgment. People will go to great lengths not to appear stupid. They will do whatever they can think to do to avoid the kind of ridicule, embarrassment and humiliation they were made to feel as a "stupid" child. Moreover, people develop quick recovery strategies for when they slip and do or say something stupid. Notice and you will see how prevalent a situation this is. Moreover, it is no wonder the "Dummy" "how to" books have been so popular. It is a relief not to have to protect oneself from self or other ridicule. Instead, a person can now feel aligned and comforted with the multitudes who need simplified direction too. (Maybe what we needed in school was simplified direction in the first place. I remember when I was being trained to be a school teacher, I was never trained in the skill of offering directions simply.)

Another significant fear of most people, especially as children, is of anger. Anger, which is frightening to witness, can be learned as a way to alleviate the discomfort of fear as well as a way to intimidate and/or control others. Sadly, The Bible is an excellent example of intimidating through the use of fear. Once anger is used successfully for the purpose intended, for example, to intimidate or control, then this self concept/belief can be born. "I am a person who enjoys feeling the power of controling others with my anger, my temper." This self concept is added to the subconscious catalogue under the heading "Methods for Controlling Others" with a cross reference "Temper Reacting Situations". These catalogued references are now available for later implementation as an 'appropriate' situation (stimulus) calls that belief into play.

Do we want to encourage governing with anger? Anger can control, can intimidate, but at what price? The types of price are rebellion, smoldering resentment, rage, volcanic eruption, and, a withering sense of self as someone other controlled. This issue of <u>source of control</u> is a critical factor. From what control source are we most empowered? With self control, of course! Many assume, however, that children need to be treated like domesticated animals, other controlled, anger/intimidation controlled. The Biblical model is of other controlled. A major Biblical tactic of control is the use of threats, and, the engendering of fear for the sake of compliance. "Spare the rod and spoil the child". When treating children in this way, many tend to rebel. Then there are those who become dis-Spirited and bent into compliance. The rebellious, the narrow minded, the dis-Spirited, and those who come to see themselves as bad or even evil, and, our world become the losers. Those in self control are the empowered. The empowered find venues for control such as alcohol and drugs generally unnecessary.

Substance abuse or any other type of self destructive conduct results from one's fears, one of which is "I don't know how to be responsible for, in control of, nor take care of myself". "I need daddy or mommy to run my life for me, like they have always insisted upon doing." "They are the only ones who know what is the right thing for me to be doing". Well meaning parents can squish the initiative out of a child, create them as dependent souls lost without them. How very prevalent and how very sad. <u>Parents need help in learning how to raise independent, responsible children</u> who actualize positive self concepts as well as positive <u>self</u> control.

Regarding the development of the self concept "evil". For hundreds of years, people have been trying to figure out how evil happens. In Christianity, the beginnings of evil are taught in the doctrine of original sin when interpreting the story of Adam and Eve. It is so ironic, how that doctrine immersed us further into fear based and evil ways. Labeling ourselves as "born in sin" and as "sinners" steeps us in it. Such self concepts can become a Petrie dish of sorts especially when combined with the additional negative self concepts and beliefs as bad and unlovable. Thus, such original sin labels nurture the very thing they were designed to control. We <u>must</u> reconstruct our concept of Eden.

Religions typically have wrestled with the origin of evil in fanciful, scary manner that exacerbates wrong doing. The truth, as opposed to frightening fantasy, can lead to the diminishment, if not the absolute demise, of evil. <u>Evil describes the behavioral consequences of our negative self concepts and beliefs.</u> Moreover, ignorance of the key negative self concepts and beliefs that foster evil consequence, have stymied resolution. Chapter 4 elucidates the most destructive of the negative self concepts and beliefs.

Our hurtful negative self concepts and beliefs more accurately constitute what is referred to as "the dark side".

We must studiously decide how to realistically nurture positive self concepts and beliefs in our children. In addition, we must learn and teach how to constructively cope with fear reactions and it's often consequent companion anger. Fear gives *immediate* access to the subconscious mind. As with a computer, "garbage in, garbage out". Would it not be better training so that it is roses in, roses out?

It is time to reverse the course of history away from what would have been the inevitable Armageddon. It is so sad that there are those who see no other way out of such potential tragedy as our world faces than by praying Armageddon happens sooner so as to witness the second coming of the Christ to save us from our currant alarming predicament. Well meaning though they may be, their prayers are about the abdication of our sacred right as a human being, our right to take responsibility, our right to grow and to make more informed choices. Wisdom comes significantly from truth seeking. I pray you will find what is here in Reconstructing Eden as wise and realize that Armageddon can be averted only if we see it for what we should never allow it to become, a self fulfilling prophecy. As you believe it so shall it be.

During the teen years, is when such self concepts as pimple face, geek, nerd, fag, weird, freak, and the latest ugly words describing our youth come into routine conversation. During the awkwardness of these teen years such references when imbedded can create havoc. Acne, by the way, often erupts more vigorously in response to the negative self concepts ugly, lazy, not good enough, unclean and/or filthy slob, and pimple faced.

As one impact from Silicon Valley, we have witnessed an unusual reversal of negative self concepts into positives as with the words geek and nerd. Those young people are now among the winners.

The teens who were raised in their earlier years to see themselves as bad, dumb, evil, and ugly, can feel tortured with vicious self identification to the additional appellations such as loser, inferior and freak. Identifying with these unfortunate words of 'teendom', which prior accumulated negative self concepts allow them to readily do, many while away their time in their rooms at home. Their rooms sometimes look like haunted caves with posters of their demented looking heros, the archetypes of their projected and ugly self concepts and beliefs. Their music choices speak to darkness and dark power for those who feel so impotent. Their games, as well as gang membership, offer the opportunity to discharge the negative energy of their fears and the rage with who they believe themselves, underneath it all, to be. These teens who often treat their bodies in unholy fashion reflect the negative self concepts and beliefs their circumstances bestowed. Gang membership reflects their sense of self as 'rejects', their need for acceptance, their need for recognition. Members hide behind tough bravado. They hide even from themselves their stark terror at feeling so unlovable, isolated, alone, and, even some that they might be gay. Subconsciously, some set it up to get themselves killed, they feel so undesirable, so unwanted. Ultimately, a child led to feel unwanted or defective in some profound manner will fulfill their parent's wishes through self abandonment which in it's ultimate form is suicide. Gang members vent their fears and rage with themselves, their predicament, their parents and the world by being at war with other gangs and with society. Their feelings of inferiority have become intolerable.

A very different scenario for self concept development during the teen years are those children who have been raised in an overly protective environment. These well meaning but fear based parents who raised their children in over protected fashion, their youngsters often become scared with the prospect of taking responsibility for themselves. They don't know how. Everything has been done for them. Subconsciously, that awareness gets translated as "I am not able to care for myself", "I'm not supposed to take care of myself, mommy and/or daddy are", etc. Then when dad says, "well son it's time for you to get a job and be on your own", the youngster freaks out internally based on his sense of inadequacy. The youngster may feel betrayed and angry because up until then the actions of his parents said he was to be dependent. What then are his options? One option is to become drunk to escape the intensely felt fear resulting from an ignorance of the skills needed to act responsibly. Another, and, not necessarily consciously derived, is to marry a gal who has been raised to see herself as a caretaker. She may have learned by the example of her mother, that a wife takes care of the husband, and from her father that a husband's role is to be dependent on his wife. That girl's beliefs fosters the attraction to the internally scared young man who needs to be taken care of. Negative history repeats itself based on the governance of one's self concepts and beliefs.

During the teen years, eating disorders generally begin to manifest and/or mobilize. For obese children, their eating related self concepts and beliefs are well entrenched, well learned from their parents and their culture. The advertising of junk foods, or invitations to mountains of food, rain on fertile ground. These children develop self concepts that include "I'm fat and I can't help it", "the more I eat the better it makes my parent(s) feel" (the 'clean plate club'), "eating great volumes of food is how you are supposed to eat", "I deserve to be humiliated and in pain for being a fat child". "I deserve to be rejected." "I am unlovable as I am." "I want to be big when I grow up." "I am lazy."

Being fat is painful. It is not fun. People hide in their fat, they punish themselves with fat, they abandon themselves by overeating, they protect themselves from being sexually approached or attacked by being fat, etcetera.

Overweight people believe they can not control their eating habits. Often, they believe they need much food to survive. Then, there are folks who are accustomed culturally to eating volumes of what are now known as fat producing foods. Loving association with certain types of food become the foods of comfort. These loving associations to food become additional negative self concepts such as "I love Mallobar cookies", or, "I love pasta", or, "I love bacon grease to season my green beans", etcetera. From whatever the sources, this accumulation of negatives relevant to that individual has to be deleted from the subconscious. It is an efficient way to empower the individual to be healthfully in control of their food choices. (See Addendum II for a more comprehensive discussion of how obesity happens.)

Young girls who become Anorexic or Bulimic, have been taught to believe, very often by their fathers, that they have to be <u>thin</u>, even to the point of <u>perfect</u> in appearance in order to be attractive to the opposite sex. Frantic subconscious fears of not being attractive enough, not lovable enough, not sexy enough fester in the demand for perfection. They literally become scared to death for fear of winding up alone and being an unattractive embarrassment to their parents. A well of terror, deepened by how they were inappropriately counseled, propel a youngster into this learned, obsessive/compulsive behavior. It is unfortunate that dads are too squeamish to explain why many men want skinny women. It isn't about looks so much as their ability to more easily perform. Men are concerned with their relative endowment sexually speaking, and how well they would be able to interact with their lover. Many men need women to be thin to get close enough to have quality of performance in terms of intercourse. Men and women need to 'fit' each other this way as well as other ways and young women need to be educated to the obvious. All men do not need skinny women. Many men are taught to want skinny women but they do not all need them to be skinny.

Now, a young woman feeling the threat of aloneness and fears of doom if not thin becomes viscerally frantic. How to get thin and remain thin become of paramount importance. Having enjoyed the comforts of food up until then compounds the problem. How to 'have your cake and eat it too' becomes the challenge to a determined to be married young woman. The solution learned from others? Binge then purge.

Frantic stuffing comes from frantic fears of having just starved oneself (to death) to be thin. Moreover, the young woman does not want to deprive herself of the pleasures of eating that she has grown accustomed to appreciating.

Throwing up deals with the frantic fear of being scared(to death) of winding up alone unless thin. It is thus that a Bulimic is created. Laxatives and severe exercise are used when the belief system of the young woman precludes vomiting or is in addition to vomiting. Obviously, laxatives and over exercise are used to 'enhance' the potential for thinness.

Anorexics can't be thin enough in order to achieve their goal of not being abandoned. Some anorexics, their goal is to have the body of a boy. In their belief system, if they look like a boy daddy will, for example, rough-house play with them as he does with a brother but not her because she is a girl.

Lucky are those teens who have cadres of positive self concepts and beliefs that guide them more easily and healthfully through the challenges of those teen years. Lucky are they to transition from being a teen into being an adult. Another of my goals with this book is to remove the luck factor and develop more systematic ways of helping children be their maximized self. <u>We, their benefactors, must 'clean house' with ourselves to bet-</u>

ter implement that goal for our children. The technology is here in this book.

During adulthood, self concept development continues. Also, negative self concept reinforcement occurs. Moreover, self concepts and beliefs can and do change. Positive changes, for example, can occur under opportune circumstance. Opportune circumstance, as opposed to structured therapeutic milieu, can happen when access to the subconscious occurs propitiously. Access to the subconscious occurs not only when hypnotized but also in a state of trauma, when anxious, and, while trancing out (self induced hypnosis). If in one of these three states a person positively reflects, "smoking is bad, I don't enjoy it, it's harming me and I don't deserve to be harmed, I am not going to be a smoker anymore", (or some words to that effect) that person has just potentially changed his/her self concept to non smoker.

Not only do self concepts change for the better, or for the worse, but new self concepts develop as well. Those who have gone to college, even for just a year, seem less into a negative self concept that they are not smart enough. Very often, those who have achieved a high school diploma, but not a college degree, they defensively react to a question regarding their academic status. These folks are defending feelings of inferiority. They suffer from a belief about themselves concerning academic inadequacy, their relative degree of 'smarts'.

Relationships with a significant other can enhance or detract from one's self concepts and beliefs. When a deeply felt relationship fails, many develop the self concept, "I am afraid of that kind of failure's pain". "I don't know if I could pull myself out again". Once those self concepts are in place, walls of one sort or another are erected. By not thinking through their plan for self protection with the conscious mind, by not delving into the consequences of their choices of defense, people don't realize that they are creating a whole cadre of different kinds of pain as a result of their solution to prevent it. There is the consequential pain of isolation, the pain of shallow one night stands, the pain of becoming fat, and, the pain of loneliness. These consequences are but a few that result from self protective barriers. (Learning pain minimization and processing skills is another goal of what is frequently referred to in this book as "core healing".)

Physical problems, emotional problems, behavioral, spiritual as well as relational problems that crop up, they all can effect our self concept development. Self concepts such as fragile, depressed, anxiety disordered, accident prone, lousy lover, unfaithful, a failure, spinster, perpetual bachelor, are but some of the negatives that can develop and/or be reinforced from younger days.

Professions also become self concepts. Artist, office manager, doctor, waiter, computer web master, etc. These self concepts can carry with them other self concepts such as obsessive compulsive, shiftless, loner, lackey, and attic dweller. Those that apply may be adopted.

During our senior years, the process of negative self concept development and reinforcement continues. The particular danger at this stage of life is the fear regarding quality of life issues, and, the reality that death is considerably closer than during even middle age. In my senior years, for example, I developed dry eye syndrome, a parched mouth while I sleep, a moderate high blood pressure, and, some elevation of cholesterol. Around the age of sixty-six, my feet, and my bones started to hurt. At times, I felt betrayed by my body with the consequent reaction called age rage. Because of my knowledge, I did not let such a situation define me as an arthritic old lady, for example. I had to turn such fear based feelings to positives. I use scary times to my advantage. Knowing that fear provides access to my subconscious, I program my 'computer center' for healing and rejuvenation. By acknowledging and then converting negative feelings and potential negative self concepts to positives provides power over them, as well as facilitating self healing. "Heal the (subconscious) mind, the body follows", even at my age. I am regenerative not arthritic. There is no way that I will allow anger to reside in my bones nor joints let alone any place else in my body because anger destroys our bodies as well as our relationships.

Summary

We now have a choice. We can design ourselves, as well as our children, to be victims of negative self concept development or it's foe. While none of us are immune to negative self concept development, the knowledge provided here can be used to minimize that potential.

My work with clients these last twenty years has been the eradication of negatives followed immediately by the replacement with positive opposite self concepts like deleting "worthless" and replacing with "worthwhile". Among other wonderful things about working with the subconscious mind is, unlike the evaluative conscious mind, it does not argue. It does not say "yes, but". It does not say, "Don't you know that I have acted worthless most of my life"? The subconscious can only implement the new self concept because the negative has been removed.

This systematic process of finding, deleting and replacing hundreds of negative self concepts with positive opposites has a profound efficacious effect on the mood, behavior and the physical well being of the individual. It frees folks to actualize their maximal potential. A future book will teach the systematic development of positive self concepts in our children.

Having dwelled here on how negative self concept development occurs is meant to forearm you. But, keep in mind, that at the same time some development of negatives occur, that throughout your life positive self concepts have developed too.

Chapter 4

Personality Reconstruction

The adage, "prevention is worth a pound of cure" applies. Be that as it may, preventing negative personality development will be a great deal easier when people who themselves have been reconstructed are those bringing children into the world. Moreover, if we really care about children, we cannot blithely proceed in having them. Without a doubt, people's psyches have absorbed religious and cultural beliefs that literally force profundity. We have been so very programed to almost heedlessly have one child after the other. Even our tax deductions encourage this profundity.

For some individuals, they are so badly programmed that subconsciously they feel sinful if they don't procreate endlessly. Recently, I worked with a woman who was symptomatic of being pregnant but was not. She had her tubes tied after birthing her second child. Being raised in a devout Catholic environment, her beliefs caused her subconscious to stimulate her body to overcome the tubal ligation's effects. The result was a false pregnancy. After reconciling the matter at the subconscious level, her sensitive, enlarged breasts and her bloated stomach returned to normal. Quite literally, she lost three-five pounds in the week following our session with no change of diet. Reiterating, "change the (subconscious) mind, the body follows".

True free will has to be championed. How we program our children's minds must be reviewed. If we act heedless of our impact upon children, we will continue to diminish them. Ignoring the information in this book would be tantamount to endorsing a living hell for most of them. (A reminder! See: "A Child's Bill of Rights" in the first Addendum at the end of this book.)

Too much is at stake to permit complacency. <u>Life itself is sacred</u>. However, <u>a sperm **nor** an egg by itself is a human life</u>. "Spilled seed" is irrelevant. Sperm, when united with egg, <u>then</u> there is life. Once there is life, <u>then</u> there has to be an equally dedicated commitment to quality of life. **<u>Quality of life must be just as sacred.</u>** When we bandwagon on a just cause, we as a country have been formidable. This cause, <u>quality of life for our children</u>, as well as for ourselves, a life free of hundreds of painful negative self concepts and beliefs, is our salvation as well as that of our world. Can you imagine self controlled, loving, giving individuals at war with each other? Not easily!

As you now know, the work of change must primarily be done person by person, one by one of us committed to <u>Reconstructing Eden</u> within ourselves. As you also now know, this work must be accomplished, must be done in the domain of the subconscious. The subconscious is boss, that is the mind that governs.

If I want to educate the client, I engage the conscious mind and it's critical faculty. And, I do want to educate my clients to these understandings. The client is encouraged to evaluate the relative efficacy of what I am saying. If they evaluate favorably, if what I say makes sense to them, then change at the subconscious level is made possible. Remember, the goal is a positive harmony of the minds so that paradise in Eden prevails. If our minds are in negative harmony, evil will prevail. It's just that simple.

We are now in a position to choose. We are no longer victims of ignorance and conjecture. We can choose that goodness and love prevail and that nastiness and fear not be tolerated. There is nothing ambiguous about it. We can be earth angels, or, agents of self and other destruction. We can birth and foster earth angels or miserable little kids who become hate filled, commit violence to themselves and/or others, as well as, act with indifference because they were treated with indifference.

Changing ourselves for the better will change our children and our world for the better. We need flounder no longer when dealing with the cross currents of life. This Chapter describes how, in the structured setting of a hypnotherapy session, "core healing" can place a person well on their way to actualizing their dreams, their potential, by resolving the problems they present for therapy. Folks would no longer be controlled by the accumulated negative self perceptions that produce their problems. Instead, as their problems evaporate, they then have the resource of preponderant, positive self concepts to use as a broader foundation upon which to build the rest of their lives. Imagine what difference the deletion of hundreds of negative self concepts and beliefs being replaced by positive ones would make in the quality of an individual's life.

In a typical psychotherapeutic setting, a client arrives with the presenting problem of a failed relationship, for example. Trained to know the various sources of a grief reaction, the psychotherapist, upon getting to know the client better, may suggest cognitive changes that they think will allevi-ate the sadness and angry feelings. These cognitive shifts, if they occur, would certainly reduce the grief reaction. However, topical therapy, such as this, misses the opportunity for "core healing".

"Core healing", additionally, would provide a healing between the client and the former lover, if not in person in the domain of the client's subcon-scious. Moreover, the negative self concepts and beliefs would be removed, those that facilitate the 'siren call' attracting that individual to the potential for another similar unhealthy relationship. People very often get divorced and find themselves involved with the same kind of person again. That potential needs to be prevented.

"Core healing" includes the further goal of programing the subcon-scious for a person's ideal mate. Without the negatives there any more, a new and more healthy 'siren call' can be programmed to occur. The client is consulted in the formulation of the traits he/she would like to be attracted to in the next relationship.

Finally, in this example, "core healing" would include pain manage-ment. People have beliefs regarding pain. It seems that many folks have negative beliefs that exacerbate painful situations. Very often too, an indi-vidual will create distancing buffers and stratagem to prevent similar pain from happening again. Some of the stratagem, a person may be aware of, yet other aspects not. To reiterate, with even the least bit of fear, a person has access to their subconscious. Unwittingly, in that moment of fear, or even when reflectively trancing out, that person can 'suggest' an idea to their subconscious to avert pain, "I'll never fall in love again." (This idea would likely occur to someone who has a prior self concept "I'm unlovable" and/or "I deserve to be abandoned anyway".) Not being aware of this whiz by thought and therefore not being able to think through this instantaneously developed idea, the individual will now become a victim of their own negative reactive decision. When implemented by the subconscious, that decision, at the very least will produce loneliness or at it's worst additional conditions such as obesity. Obesity has been the stratagem of choice for conservatively hundreds of thousands of people around the world. At least, those numbers would be my guess. And, these types of consequences, formulated to prevent one kind of pain, will now produce a whole other kind of pain. This ill devised stratagem can be reversed if the psychotherapist has been trained in the use of and has a commitment to "core healing". In fancy language, I call such thorough process "systematic neuro linguistic reprogramming". (I used to call what I do Laser Regression Hypnotherapy but subsequently, over time, others took over this concept and adjusted it for their own purposes.) As an aside, this type of "core healing" seems to repair any negatively altered regions or processes of the brain.

Most, if not all, psychotherapists will tell you the incredible importance of Cognitive Therapy. So would I. Cognitive Therapy refers to the helpful effect when a person's self concepts are changed for the better through a process of reframed thinking. The goal is changing a negative idea to a positive. That goal is just as key to "core healing". However, when using the hypnotherapeutic process about to be described here in more detail, Cognitive Therapy is profoundly more helpful to the client when the therapist does not have to guess, but knows how to find the negative self concepts in need of adjustment. (Traditionally trained therapists have studied and have actual lists of typical self concepts that they select for change, on a case by case basis. That is certainly a helpful step. Be that as it may, the actual knowledge of the beliefs in need of change are in the client not the psychotherapist.)

The goals of what is referred to here as "core healing" are these:

- the amelioration of all of a person's presenting problems either emotional, physical, relational, behavioral, and/or Spiritual to the best that we (the client and the therapist as a team) can achieve;

- healing the hurt child, teenaged youth, and, the adult selves injured by life circumstance;

- healing hurtful relationships including with God;

- creating templates at the subconscious level of assertive, adult to adult conduct as needed by the circumstance of a particular client an example of which is constructive anger management;

- identifying all of a person's fears and removing them (typical fears include: being alone; the unknown; being responsible (especially in the sense of being at fault); being stupid; pain; being unlovable; rejection; not being good enough; etc.);

- removing negative emotion from where ever it resides within the organs or body parts of an individual;

- helping an individual to the "aha" phenomenon…."so that is why I have this or that problem". This revelation of <u>exact</u>, as opposed to approximate truth, and, the exhilarated feeling of the 'aha', provides immediate conquest over the problem(s) presented for amelioration.

- creating ease in managing pain;

- transforming a person from worrier (an expert at "stinkin thinkin") to a person who, when a <u>concern</u> arises, now develops and implements a flexible plan of resolution;

- desensitizing negative memories;

- treating unhealthy coping styles such as smoking, eating too much, the misuse of drugs and alcohol, etcetera by removing as many of a person's negative self concepts and beliefs, significant ones of which are in the form of fears, that then, I would speculate, adjusts brain chemistry and symmetry for the better;

- enhancing the client's knowledge of God, if they so desire; and,

- assuring that clients are not actualizing any of the following negative self concepts. (Consciously, there are very few who are aware that they are implementing these negative self concepts. <u>**Subconsciously,** and quite probably, **most of us** are implementing some or all of these to some degree.</u> I deem number one below to be the most dangerous, the second one exceedingly damaging and number six profoundly debilitating to the potential for quality life and peace on earth.)

1. I deserve to be abandoned by others, self and God

2. I deserve to be punished; and, punishment changes bad behavior.

3. I'm not good enough. Examples: not smart enough, not pretty enough etc.

4. I'm bad, worthless, weak, lazy, shy, unimportant, scared, angry, inadequate, unlovable, unworthy of unconditional love, inferior, a failure, loser, stupid, coward, afraid of pain, unable to take care of myself, afraid of responsibility for myself or for a child, nervous, stressed (out of control), a "bad seed", depressed, etc.

5. I have to be perfect (do everything just right). The pursuit of excellence is far healthier.

6. I'm <u>not</u> supposed to be in control of myself. (Everyone in authority in my life is supposed to be.) <u>Many</u> of these folks become other or outside source controlled individuals.

7. I'm afraid to be alone.

8. I'm helpless, powerless.

These negative self concepts as reconfiguring constellations can become most if not all of the personality disorders. Moreover, they lead to addictions, suicide, insanity, early or excessive child bearing, the mood disorders, divorce, high blood pressure, cancer, asthma, heart disease, autoimmune disease, etc. My experience also suggests that Schizophrenia seems to result from the extreme of number six above which leads to a need for delusions of grandeur (power), the auditory delusions of controlling companions and an intense fear regarding their relative competence to take care of themselves. Moreover, Schizophrenics do not seem to be raised in homes that tend to model wholesome, smooth social skills. There is usually at least one <u>exceedingly</u> domineering, snoopy parent. The snoopy part leads to paranoia. And, number one · above contributes to the Schizophrenic's social isolation and feelings of not being lovable. Finally, when there is the abandonment of God, literally, it can take the light out of a Schizophrenic's eyes. They go dark. Moreover, the abandonment of God can thrust one into the stark terror of nothingness, total aloneness, and helplessness that are key precursors to insanity.

"I can't handle it anymore" are five of the most dangerous words out of a person's mouth. Those words lead to insanity too. A person takes a mental vacation (self abandonment)so as to be taken care of by someone else. Self abandonment in the extreme= suicide.

I can't emphasize strongly enough, that our children need to be raised, as best we can, without the key negative self concepts indicated in numbers one through eight above. But once imbedded, thank God, there is now a way out by a dedication to <u>Reconstructing Eden</u>, the restructuring of the negative aspects of a person's personality.

Personality restructuring suggests an umbrella psychotherapeutic goal. It is about what I call "cleaning house". Granted, a client presenting themselves for therapy due to a grief reaction resulting from a failed relationship would be thrilled to have their talk therapist or even their hypnotherapist help them over it. But, would it not, as discussed earlier, be more thrilling for such clients to not only put behind them any over reaction to their loss but be positioned to not become attracted to the same type of person again? And, not only that, wouldn't they be thrilled to be unburdened of other negative self concepts and beliefs fostering other of their problems? When one invests in a comprehensive make over, psychologically speaking, hopefully all fears are found and deleted which heightens self confidence. The net effect of this 'cleaned house' is a centered, healthier, self controlled, happy individual.

This hypnotherapeutic process has also been developed to once and for all heal old traumas. Those traumas involve perpetrators. I call these perpetrators a person's cast of characters. Everyone of those relationships need to be dealt with in forgiving fashion. Pain and anger are essential to be released from a person's body for the sake of his/her health and sense of well being. Healing the relationships of those who have hurt my client is a must whether it be, mom, dad, stepfather, stepmother, a grandparent, a teacher, a swim coach, etc. My goal is to foster peace. The process encourages, demonstrates, and, imprints healthy anger management, assertive, compassionate adult to adult interaction. The process is also geared to heal the younger selves of the client. A significant portion of the healing phase needs to be done with them. They are the ones bringing their anxieties and childish rebellion into the now of an adult's experience. For example, a client presented with the problem of nearly passing out from a panic attack at the first staff meeting he was to conduct. His conscious mind pushed on him to stay put and do his job. His subconscious stimulated his adrenal and other glands to facilitate flight. Their was an intra psychic battle being waged. The more the conscious mind fought the urge to run, the more adrenaline that was pumped into his system creating a literal feeling of imbalance to the point he had to sit down to keep from falling over. Why was there a child self within telling him to run? Using a hypnotherapeutic technique called age regression, I asked the individual's subconscious to take us back to the most critical the most relevant memory to the question: Why did I get a panic attack at the staff meeting?

Under hypnosis, the <u>relevant</u> memory that came up was from when he was in second grade. His teacher called him to the chalk board to solve a math problem. He made a mistake. His teacher, egregiously said, "sit down stupid". The boy's classmates broke out laughing. In that moment of trauma, the window to his subconscious flew open. The boy reacted to this trauma. Now, in the presence of his subconscious, he made a host of what I call negative reactive decisions as a result of what happened. They became more of his negative self concepts and beliefs. These negatives came into play as the staff meeting approached.

If he had some appropriately foundational positive self concepts and beliefs, this client might well have made some positive reactive decisions instead. An example of that kind of reaction would be this thought: "mom is good with the times tables." "I'll get her to drill me so the next time the teacher calls upon me I will be ready." Now, who has he become as a result of this reactive decision? <u>He is a person who does his homework</u>. And in the overall scheme of things, being a person who does home work is a positive self concept. We know, however, that his reactive decisions were negative because of his panic attack at the staff meeting.

At lightening speed, in the presence of his subconscious, this client, like thousands of others who feel intimidated to perform in front of an audience, made reactive decisions like: performing in front of a group is dangerous; I can't trust myself not to come across as stupid; I must deserve to be embarrassed and humiliated when performing in front of a group; I don't want to be in a situation like that again; and, there is a part of me that feels like I am stupid. Now, this man finds himself in conflict. He is thrilled about his promotion as a manager, but not so thrilled because it requires that he conduct a weekly staff meeting. Not consciously recalling the second grade incident, he may wonder why he dreads the staff meeting part. He may simply rationalize, "well hardly anybody likes performing in front of a group, I'm just one of them". However, he could not simply dismiss this rationalization because of the panic attack. He was forced to come to grips with what was actually going on.

Being governed by the negative self concepts having to do with performing in front of a group, as the time to present himself before his staff drew near, he reported the physiological manifestations of anxiety such as sweaty palms, an increased heart rate and starting to hyperventilate. His subconscious was already putting out an 'appropriate' response to the 'danger' of the upcoming meeting where he would be positioned in front of the group. His negative self concepts and beliefs were culled from the archives. They produced the logical flight response. His conscious mind, unaware of this historical influence and how it produced the physiological consequence, could not make sense out of the anxiety he felt. And, for fear of not doing his job, he forced himself to stay put in front of the group. This decision caused the subconscious to put out more fright/flight hormones in the body which then created the chemically induced physical turmoil called a panic attack.

To recap! There was a <u>stimulus</u>(the staff meeting). The subconscious pulled from the archives all relevant self concepts and beliefs. These were interpreted by the subconscious. The interpretation? There is impending and soon to be immediate danger. Reaction? Flee! To assist with self protective flight, the subconscious arranged for the release of body stimulants to facilitate hyper vigilance and energized <u>response. That is an anatomy of a panic attack.</u>

To fix such a problem requires not just the change of the negative self concepts into positive, but the desensitization of the memory. What does that mean? While in hypnosis, with access to the subconscious, the client will be guided into an assertive, adult to adult confrontation with his second grade teacher imprinting the constructive discharge of his anger. It can be considered constructive because the client is caused to speak to the teacher without hostility nor expletives. Moreover, he expresses the hurtful consequences of her conduct to his child self that day. All the while, the client is positioned not as a child but rather as a mature adult. Now with appropriate perspective, fault for the event is placed where it belongs, and, allows for forgiveness of self for making a mistake that caused him ridicule, and, of the teacher for her mistakes, thus healing an old wound once and for all. By the way, keep in mind that all forgiveness means is the releasing of pain and anger, a point I stress with every client before conducting "core healing". Forgiveness does not mean condoning.

My experience indicates that pain and anger feelings are housed in various places in the body. Where in the body depends on the self concepts and beliefs of the individual. The retention of pain and anger in the body happens because a person is not generally taught that it can be released nor how to release it.

Pain and anger produce disease such as high blood pressure, enlarged knuckles, heart attacks, cancer, etcetera. "Core healing", among other things, calls for the release from the body of all damaging emotion stored there. Under hypnosis, this emptying of negative emotion becomes easy. It can be suggested to the subconscious to scan the body to locate these unhealthy emotional deposits. Once located, they can be 'washed' clear of the body. Healing suggestions are then offered to heal the irritated joints, stomach lining, heart rending, etc. Generally, I use something as unimaginative yet profoundly meaningful as a healing radiant flowing light that washes through every pore and cell of a person's body. Remember, the subconscious mind is an amoral entity. It makes no value judgements. So unless there are conflicting beliefs, which by the time this procedure occurs there are considerably fewer, then these healing suggestions are free to be implemented. (If there were any potential for conflicting beliefs, that notion would already have been registered by the therapist during the intake procedure where medical problems of any sort are identified.)

"Core healing" also calls not only for mature imprinting of constructively expressed anger but, in this case, a rehearsal staff meeting. Again, in the domain of the subconscious, this client was guided to witness himself assertively conducting a staff meeting. Fortunately, as a therapist, it was easy for me to conjure an appropriately led staff meeting based on my experience as a former administrator. He was imprinted with not only the words but the images related to assertively conducting his next staff meeting. Thus, he was given the automatic knowledge to draw upon, and, the readiness to use it with self confidence. With this assertive rehearsal, he had already experienced himself successfully conducting the staff meeting. Moreover, his self concept had thereby become adept at conducting staff meetings. Consequence? Feelings of confidence plus readiness to perform!

Just as we are not able to do transplant surgery on ourselves, we cannot transplant loving, healthy, strengthening self concepts and beliefs into ourselves. We may create positive mantras, try our best to think positively, put a list of positive reinforcers on our mirror, do self hypnosis and yet remain blocked because of the over-riding effect of any unknown, undeleted negative self concepts and beliefs. At last, we can become **un**blocked in service of becoming not only free of our problems but free to become a maximized self as discussed in the next chapter.

To summarize! Metaphorically speaking, <u>first</u> each of our cancerous <u>fears and negative self concepts and beliefs must be identified,</u> not by guess work, but by knowing how to ferret the truth from the subconscious of an individual by using a variety of hypnotherapeutic techniques. <u>Then,</u> <u>these</u> enervating <u>fears</u> that so often lead to blind anger <u>plus the</u> ensuing development of <u>self defeating self concepts must be dissolved</u>. No matter where in the body of an individual that they reside, <u>the negatives must be transplanted with positive opposites</u>. <u>Moreover, the cancer enhancing memories</u> that produced the negatives <u>need to be reframed</u> so they nourish a person's sense of self, as opposed to allowing them the opportunity for multiplying the fears and negatives that drain away one's life. This is the elaborate, efficient process that I am sharing with you in this book. In fancy language alluded to earlier, it is a systematic process of neuro-linguistic reprogramming that results in the neurological rewiring of the brain. In computer terms, it is a process of 'defragging'. It also replaces old software with an updated version. In Spiritual terms, it is a journey to Wisdom, the kind that results in feeling free and unburdened through truths discovered and healthfully, forgivingly addressed. This is the only way negative history will be prevented from repeating itself from generation to generation. Therefore, let us become legion in <u>Reconstructing Eden</u>.

To <u>Reconstruct Eden</u>, we must deal with truth not simply conviction. I can not say absolutely that everything I have said is exactly correct. I have been in private practice not in a research setting. As a scientist, and the field of psychology is a science, we are taught early on in our training to be cautious when speaking in certainties. "It seems that", is a common prefatory phrase. Be that as it may, nineteen years of experience, with often extraordinary results, does carry weight.

Based upon success after success, as has been measured with pre/post testing on the Minnesota Multiphasic Personality Inventory 2 (the updated version), it <u>seems that</u>, personality can be constructively changed. On *average*, for most clients, the process described here takes ten and a half to fourteen *hours* of work over a period of about six to eight weeks.

How can personality, that took years to forge, be adjusted so quickly? First of all what is being reconstructed are only the negative aspects. Obviously, we want to keep and honor the positive. Also, it helps to work with the client in a team play effort yet one where they are 'boss'. The therapist is a professional facilitator of constructive change, changes the client has chosen to make. We work with the understanding that to the best of our ability, we are going to identify all of that individual's problems, and agree together to 'clean house' thoroughly. Moreover, I teach my clients how to get into a new habit, the habit of positive thinking and then provide them the self concept foundation to succeed.

The process used is structured for thoroughness. Truth seeking is essential. And, if you believe quite truly, that it will work for you, then it will. We will want to know, in fact, all the reasons why you have those x and y and z problems. Fixing problems becomes easy once the truth, the whole truth and nothing but the truth is dealt with in unremitting fashion. People enjoy the revelations about why they actually do what they do, people love putting the puzzle of self together, they relish the 'aha' phenomenon, the reaction, "so that is why I actually do what I do". It provides such a freeing, uplifted feeling.

What also distinguishes this work, is that the therapist's goal is not to simply address the presenting problem. The medical model, upon which we in the field of psychology have leaned, goes something like this. Got a broken leg? Then the doctor deals with relevant aspects of that person's physiological history, he/she evaluates the fracture, and, then decides the best course of action necessary for repair. An MRI is done or x-rays are taken, the leg is reset, skin sewn, a cast put on, etc. In other words, the leg is repaired, end of story. Similarly, with many of my colleagues in the mental health field.

A person presents with a phobia. An intake is conducted by the psychotherapist. Relevant history examined. The therapist contracts with the client for treatment after explaining what is the plan of resolution. The client agrees. The therapist proceeds and let us assume succeeds. The client says "thank you". The therapist responds, "my pleasure, and, if anything else comes up know that I am here to help". The client leaves satisfied. The phobia is gone. End of story!

The same person, if they called me, would receive a different psychotherapeutic invitation. Briefly, I would explain about what I do and indicate that I only work with those agreeing to 'cleaning house' meaning we are going to remove approximately two to four hundred negative self concepts and beliefs and replace with positive opposites. Also, we are going to heal old wounds, achieve constructive control over their mind and behavior, give them the power to implement positive thinking, and, come to terms with the significant relationships in their lives. While more expensive than the medical model, which I refer to as psychotherapeutic band aide work, I explain that I have a way to foster peace within themselves, get rid of <u>all</u> their fears, heighten their self confidence, give them constructive control over any and all of their self defeating behaviors, feel centered, interact with family members better, etc. However, I always hasten to add the obvious, "I am not God", and while I'll try to fix perfectly every problem a person has, please know that may not happen. Be that as it may, the process I have embellished over the last nineteen years does succeed rather well with most clients. Obviously, there are those with whom I fail completely or some just so-so.

The forgoing is a heck of a lot to promise people. The process and the knowledge presented here delivers, and, I can prove it. When working at a psychiatric hospital in their eating disorder unit, I showed the Executive Director amazing Minnesota Multi-Phasic Personality 2 pre therapy post therapy test results for several of the patients from the unit. My take on his unenthusiastic response was that he was not interested in emptying beds just filling them. And, as an aside, from what some colleagues who are astute in using hypnosis have reported of their experience in prisons, they too got 'the cold shoulder' even though they were succeeding with so many inmates. A prison nurse I met affirmed that where she worked they drug inmates until their release. High recidivism and the cost of medications are not cheaper. I pray that based upon what you are learning here that the idea of correction centers is taken much more seriously, as opposed to being punishment facilities. My work suggests that *punishment has been one of the most destructive forces ever created by man*. I put it right up their with the menace to our current civilization that are the terrorists. Both are the result of feelings of outrage and impotence. We have been unfortunately programmed to believe and therefore our subconscious can cause us to experience that punishment assuages pain, feelings of helplessness as well as betrayed feelings. What we have not been taught is that we savage ourselves as the performer of the punishment. Yes, sequester those souls who are of harm to themselves and others but why brutalize them further? And, why not reduce recidivism with this or some other form of "core healing" that works for a lot of people, even those diagnosed as having some degree of an Antisocial Personality Disorder? It is so very much cheaper.

Chapter 5
The Maximized Self

To be at peace within ourselves at last…what marvelous news! To change our personalities, once thought immutable, wow! "Wow" is what so many of my clients exclaim, at the conclusion of a personality altering session. The psychotherapeutic process I learned nineteen years ago and have embellished and use ever since delivers awesome results for so many. This process can reconstruct Eden, and bring one back, in a sense, to the original conception.

A result of reconstruction is a client's freedom to choose to become a maximized, loving, content individual who is free to be an ambassador of peace by actualizing gentle loving kindness. Success, for those who make such a choice, takes on new meaning. It is <u>not</u> like one of my male clients said to me many years ago. He said, "the guy that wins, the guy that gets the touchdown in front of cheering crowds is the guy with the most money." Actually, that guy loses because accumulating money competitively results in pyrrhic victory. Greed must be his way of life. Power derived in that way never slakes thirst.

Authentic winners may earn a lot of money but their focus is not just on accumulation. They use their talents, abilities, wealth and power in a way to serve others. A person like Oprah Winfrey, now there is a real life grid-iron hero.

Maximized individuals:

Honor Diversity

Honoring diversity, as a concept, means one has the freedom according to their belief system to respect the rights and differences of others. Honoring diversity does not mean having to accept nor actualize those differences. To honor diversity simply means an openness, an intellectual availability to new and/or different ideas, styles, and ways of behaving. It's a respectfulness of the differences. When there is disagreement with the difference, maximized individuals do not run roughshod over the 'offending' person or group. Understanding and compassionate response are the hallmarks rather than, in the following example, horrified castigation. It is easy to experience horror at a Hannibal Lecter. Moreover, it is quite appropriate to confine such an individual away from society. The challenge here is compassionate treatment rather than copying in some form or other the man's savagery. Compassionate treatment would honor diversity even in it's most repugnant form.

(Remember, when you read Chapter 4, that the correction of conduct even of a criminal nature is now doable. For all criminals? No, some seem too far gone. That is one reason why the prevention inherent in correcting ourselves *before* we parent becomes such a critical factor.

Unwittingly, we can develope the kinds of self concepts that lead to fraudulent, violent, irreverent behavior)

Walk Humbly

Arrogance is the manner of a person who is defending feelings of inferiority. Arrogance also derives from an inappropriately elevated sense of self where, for example, one's parents raise a child with the child being the center of their universe rather than God. The child grows up wanting to protect the comfort of this exaggerated form of self importance. It feels very secure. The headiness of this secure power position leads to a negative reactive decision to protect this position based on what can be an intense fear, for it's loss. Obviating the loss of limelight, pomposity reigns and the ugliness of such demeanor, the distastefulness of such pomposity becomes lost to his purview. Quite literally, subconsciously,a person can become scared to death for loss of position.

Walking humbly is evidence of comfortableness with position neither feeling inferior nor needing to act superior. A humble individual bows with humility in the presence of our Lord as well as bowing to the accomplishments of others. Competition, for the sake of surmounting feelings of inadequacy seems wrong and irrelevant.

Think Independently

'Thinking outside the box' is one's ability to be creative and inventive. When, as children, if we are raised like a marine recruit, this ability is considerably minimized if not, in fact, squashed. Children are not soldiers and must not be raised by martinets. Narrow mindedness at the least and even murderous impulsiveness results. Think about Columbine and think about the self concept of a child raised in military fashion. That <u>child</u> becomes, self conceptually, a soldier. What do soldiers do? They kill their enemies, indiscriminately, in fact, just as many killed as possible. Imagine this youngster coming to believe the other kids at school are not his friends. They are his enemies. Things are now ripe for a military plan to be formulated and executed. Probably in the mind of such a youngster is that such an action might even make him a hero, at least in the eyes of other beleaguered teens. High school can be hell for those not in the 'in' group. While it could be argued that conceiving the plan was done with independent thinking, actually, it was not. The plan rigidly conformed to the militaristic model.

Seek Truth

People who are active seekers of truth have learned to confront the full range of their feelings, are knowledge thirsty and tend to be free of corruption emotionally, physically, behaviorally, relationally, and, Spiritually. They do not readily slide into a coping style of denial. Being in touch with one's actual feelings and learning how to constructively discharge them is an embraced skill. That ability offers the freedom of enhanced self control.

Truth seeking avoids engaging in subterfuge. Moreover, seeking out truth no matter how obscure or how fraught with controversy is a commitment to those embracing the concept of freedom, the kind that only actual truth can provide.

Foster Self (versus other) Control

Self controlled individuals do not need somebody or something outside themselves to control nor navigate their life for them. Characteristically, they are good team players, physically healthy, success oriented, and, often engage marriage as a partnership.

Characteristically, those who have not learned self control generally experience a different model of control in their homes. Their parents model control or be controlled styles of interacting. One or both parents act weak, dependent and acquiescent. Some homes offer a combination of inept styles. Also, parents who have a desperate need to be the perfect parent, model extremely controlling involvement in the lives of their children. In order for a parent to be the perfect mom or dad means that their children have to be aces too. Trying to be perfect stresses out children as well as their parents. These parents tend to over control their children rather than have a disciplinary program ready from the get-go to nurture the child's self control.

One or both parents, when trying to be perfect, act with supreme control over the child which usually becomes a psychological disaster in the form of Cyclothymia, if not Bi Polar Disorder, the Eating Disorders, Obsessive Compulsive Disorder, Anxiety Disorder, and, some degree of Depression that can lead to suicide. I call "perfectionism" a disease that infects and robs an individual of serenity. Excellence is a far better and more realistic human standard.

Over controlled children are generally intimidated to behave and are coerced into dependency. In the extreme, I believe this is a significant contributing factor to Schizophrenia.

Poor parental models of self control, produce threats, implied or expressed plus the implementation of one form of punishment or another. Some families exhibit models of horrendous violence as well as out of control, anti social conduct in the extreme. Children come to believe this is the way to interact. The old heartwarming movies and such wonderful television series as <u>The Waltons</u> and <u>The Little House on The Prairie</u> are far too scarce in today's world. We need to give youngsters opportunities to view healthy family interaction.

Children who lack aspects of self control become adults who are either controllers and/or needy of being controlled by sources outside of themselves. The over controlled as well as the neglected, usually develop addictions of one sort or another and generally are quite self and/or other punitive in either overt or covert fashion. (We need to closely examine the difference between the effects of punishment, which is other control, and those taught self control.)

We can not and must not gnash our teeth at parents who have failed in these ways. It is not their fault. They were raised similarly just as were their parents and on back throughout the history of human kind. Rather, it is our responsibility to take the information in this and other similar books to heart, create a plan of betterment over the coming decades and get started. My next book will be geared to fostering that goal.

(See Addendum One at the end of this book entitled: A Child's Bill of Rights.)

Hone and Give of their Gifts

Life is so much more joyous when we are raised to be caring individuals who are guided so as to use our uniqueness(es) in service of others. We become less dependent on recognition outside ourselves and more self encouraging when we become this kind of person.

A maximized individual finds comfort in being of service to others. This kind of individual takes their specialness as a person, their unique talents and abilities, hones and uses these gifts in celebratory service, in one way or another, of all that is living. Take a hydrocephalic child who, raised lovingly, and is athletically inclined, how they inspire us when they compete in their very own Olympic games.

Unfortunately, too many of us are blinded to our purpose to the extent we dwell in our fears and negativity. We lose our drive and our power in service of our fears. An example would be of a young woman who because she was not made cognizant of her assets, not educated to promote their use, raised with a sense of unworthiness, develops fears around her inadequacies. Imagine also, that this very same woman feels exempt from God's presence and keenly fears being alone. What might such a person do?

Marry the first guy she can snag and promptly get pregnant so as to address her various fears. Result? Negative history is perpetuated.

(For study: Sexual drive and/or one's fears and/or one's unquestioned beliefs regarding life's purpose to be a mother produce human babies not maternal instinct. However, their care seems maternally instinctual.)

Eschew Fear and Ugly Anger

The power for making sound choices is incredibly enhanced by the freedom from fear. One's fears engender an assortment of negative self concepts and beliefs that create stumbling blocks. Unwittingly, a person's culture, their milieu, their family, their religion, their community, their country, our world engenders a host of negatives. These fears, these negatives are interfering with our serenity and our rich self-actualization as the beautiful creatures we have it in us to be.

We can become educated through the plethora of wonderful self-help books, but not too often are we able to assert ourselves in the ways we have learned we would prefer. That is where the type of psychotherapy discussed in this book comes into play. People who free themselves of their negativity can then act in the assertive manner they learn about but have been blocked from achieving.

Regarding anger, it is taught and/or it is simply felt as a consequence. We learn to do overt or covert anger against others as well as self. Anger is taught to be loudly ugly, or passive/aggressively exhibited or not in ugly fashion. Anger is often used to intimidate/control/punish others as well as to exhaust pent up emotion especially fear energy. Anger, after all, arises primarily from fear, as well as from the underlying fears inherent in feelings of unjust treatment, and/or, disappointment in self.

Love Unconditionally

Those who love unconditionally, love themselves that way as well as others. These individuals would not consider abandoning themselves nor those they love. These people acknowledge their weaknesses and their strengths. In that moment of observation, they accept themselves as good enough recognizing that is all they can be right then. Also, in that moment, they are free to challenge themselves by identifying their next growth step. Life, for those who love unconditionally, is a journey of becoming, of growing, of respectfulness, of exhibiting grace, warmth of style and ease of manner.

Act Meekly

Acting meekly means being among the gentle and the kind. With true and earnest endeavor, being among the meek is one of the best decisions about who to be that a person can ever make. There are appropriate times for being tough and rugged but being meek need not necessarily be compromised in the process. The self disciplines of the East, as in some of their martial arts, can teach such co-existence.

Forgive Readily

Forgiveness means letting go of pain and anger. Be the fastest forgiver in town. It is agonizing and depressing wallowing in pain and anger. We have the power inherent in our choices to minimize duration and intensity of pain. We are not helpless in its management. Nor need we be victims helplessly absorbing ugly anger. Ugly anger that sidesteps forgiveness is a self indulgent, learned bad habit, geared to cause pain sometimes in the attempt to relieve one's own. Relieve your pain and angers instead through forgiveness. Ask for it, and it is Given. Allow yourself to ask for, to receive, and, to readily offer authentic forgiveness.

Embrace Responsibility Fully

The mark of maturity is the welcoming of responsibility versus fearing it. People very often flee being responsible because their experience with it has been negative. For them being responsible often meant being to blame or at fault. Children, raised punitively, deeply fear being at fault because of their experience with harsh consequence. If instead of parental ire, children were given parental <u>time</u> to learn from a mistake, to learn from their misbehavior, growth would take place. Fear would not as likely be associated with failure or mistakes. Consequently, taking responsibility for oneself would feel appropriate and strengthening.

People also fear responsibility because they do not, either consciously or subconsciously, view themselves as capable nor adequately competent to do so. Or, as children, they were inappropriately burdened with responsibilities. There are those parents who have over burdened a child with supervisory responsibility, for example, over a younger sibling. There are also those parents who unwittingly make their children feel responsible for themselves and their happiness. Burdening a child with such expectation also develops into a fear of overload, a feeling of pressure that can readily lead to feelings of resentment, being out of control and thus into feelings of depression.

Then there are those who take on responsibilities that are not theirs to take. They were raised to believe that is what they are supposed to do. For them embracing responsibility fully is easy but those folks need help in differentiating between appropriate and inappropriate arenas in which to do so. For example, taking responsibility for someone else's happiness while it sounds noble, actually, it is unfair. It robs that individual of learning how to be responsible for generating his or her own happiness. Contributing to the happiness of others is different than taking responsibility for it.

Want to Grow and Improve

Living life as a never ending journey of 'growing up', releases us from the pressure of having to be "all grown up" by the unrealistic age of twenty-one. Moreover, it makes life far more enjoyable not to place unrealistic expectations upon ourselves. Wanting to grow and improve can become an inviting aspect of life's journey. Growing and improving produces it own pleasure, it's own rewards.

Dwell in Goodness

Goodness is more likely next to Godliness than cleanliness. Cleanliness is good. Goodness is even better. Seeing ourselves as basically and fundamentally good is <u>absolutely</u> essential to ease of relationship with God. Viewing ourselves in any other way tends to produce distance.

Act with Integrity

When we do what is right, what is just, what is honest on a consistent basis, we enjoy admiration and wholesome respect from self to self and from others to self. Those who are totally antisocial, resoundingly reject being caring most likely because they were so blatantly not cared about. They have come to view life cynically and reject integrity as the game plan of fools. Those void of commitment to social principles live in a world of volcanic emptiness. Undoubtably, they and their fundamental goodness were terribly rejected.

Make Choices Wisely

If we expect children to hone their ability at making wise choices, we as adults must model that process. Teaching children how to do so will position them for constructive self control as well as for success.

Making choices wisely involves information gathering, identifying the various courses of action in response to the situation, assessing the pros and cons of a given decision by looking for anticipated consequences regarding the various aspects of the decision. Then, the plan is implemented. If it needs modifying along the way, it can be. If the plan should be abandoned, it can be. Moreover, if necessary, a Plan B can be generated.

Foster Equality

Yin and yang, black, white, pink, brown, yellow, beige; honored, they enrich. Denigrated differences destroy. Ignorance and fear of differences rends.

Treasure Freedom

Freedom from negativity is the elixir of the soul. Truth is essential to freedom.

Honor God

Biblically, unfortunately, we are taught to "fear" rather than be "in awe of" God. The ancient Hebrew word can be translated either way. Why did the earliest Biblical editors choose fear? Fear controls, weakens and enslaves while love and awe strengthens. Was that the purpose to control through fear? Or, was it ignorance as to the tortuous outcomes of horrifying images and concepts? Fear, as the mode to control, is the tool of fools. Ultimately, it generates an ugly sense of self. Oh yes, there can be delicious feelings of power. However, the price to others and self makes the use of fear as a weapon with which to control intolerable and exhausting.

God, the Greatest Lover of all time, and, Jesus, the Lamb, the Shepard who is the reflection of such extraordinary love frequently, Biblically, are painted as wrathful, punitive, and destructive. I see myself as a champion of their tender mercies.

The knowledge necessary for what my clients call "core healing", has been shared with you the reader in this book. That knowledge has irrevocably led me from being oh so judgmental to being a woman of compassion. That same and even more encompassing knowledge can only have led to Their enormous compassion for each and every one of us. My work, as a psychotherapist, irrefutably indicates that there is a Magnificent, Unconditionally Loving, Master plan afoot with which to achieve our salvation. The Bible, as it is, is not it. For example, from a Spiritual and psychological perspective, The New Testament book entitled Revelation should be deleted altogether, just as much of Noah's story in The Old Testament. It is so antithetical to the Majesty of our loving God. Those who must have edited the original documents to form of The Bible used horrific metaphors and concepts with which to explain what was not understood. Also, the horrific aspects of it seem designed to manipulate people through fearful concepts and images. We cannot allow ourselves to be the unhealthy victims of such demagoguery. Propounding such fearsomeness does, in fact, generate negative self concepts and beliefs within us that we then actualize to our own and societies' detriment.

The Holy Bible, as it is, needs retirement from hierarchical position in our lives. Editing it, as I have done, to create The Loving Bible would be immeasurably helpful to our psyches. My work is founded on the concept, "as you believe it so shall it be". If we believe in a cataclysmic Armageddon, we will generate it. As mentioned earlier, we are already well on our way. It is that old 'self fulfilling prophecy' at work.

The Loving Bible seems so much more appropriate to the reality of the Loving God and his son Jesus the rabbi, the healer, the emissary. The studiousness and the ethical principals of Judaism, the compassionate teachings of Jesus, and, the enlightenment derived from Buddhism are what a maximized individual is all about. We cannot fritter away time with issues regarding proselytization of a particular religion. Rather, it is important to learn from the compassion and love enhancing teachings of other religions. Accumulate all wholesome concepts in a mental notebook entitled The Best and Most Loving Teachings from The World's Religions. Such teachings can expand our awareness and immeasurably help in leading us into enlightenment and just conduct. The process described in this book reconstructs an individual so as to be able to live and act in such enlightened form.

Pursue Peace

Peace in our world will happen by each of us transcending our warring histories especially within our own beings. In so doing, we withdraw the menacing protrusion of our negativity into the lives of others. Our Messianic delivery has arrived. The loving teachings of such greats as Christ and Buddha can be actualized and so much more readily through a commitment to "core healing" and to the personal growth goal to maximize the self in these ways. Then we immeasurably enhance the potential for real peace. Let us be the be the collective messiah. That's the ticket to quality life ever lasting. Then there will be peace. Together, one by one of us, we can choose to make it happen.

Addendum I

A Child's Bill of Rights

Others have written such a list as the one that follows. Mine was written a number of years ago. I remember sharing it with a retired Editor of The Miami Herald who was dedicating his retirement years to the welfare of children.

Though perhaps not entirely different than someone else's version, the concept is so incredibly important that it should be ever at the forefront of our minds. Just as we honor our country's Bill of Rights, honor these rights as just as sacred.

Before deciding to become pregnant, imagine hearing an about to be conceived child whispering in your ear, and saying, "please think of my needs before your own"."Before proceeding in unprotected fashion, remember that I deserve:

- to be born into a family where the parents are in a stable, loving relationship. Parents who are in destructive relationship, parents who are screaming and fighting with each other will create such agitation and fear within me that Attention Deficit Disorder or Attention Deficit and Hyperactivity Disorder will likely result. Not only that, I would grow up ready to act just like you did because you were my template. I would come to believe that such ugly interaction is how one conducts themselves when married.

- <u>to be really wanted, loved and treated with affection by both my parents.</u> When one or both of you resent my existence and treats me indifferently, I will learn to feel cold and indifferent towards myself and others. I may come to want to please you by hastening my departure from this world. Why do you think little tykes commit suicide?

- <u>to be treated respectfully and gently.</u> Parents, who openly or with stealth abuse their children raise children, who can become abusers of their children and/or grow up actualizing the belief that they deserve to be abused. **Children's minds interpret themselves as the fault.** If a child is treated badly, their immature logic translates the situation as, "I must be bad, for being treated that way."

- <u>to be prized no matter what the configuration of my genitalia.</u> I must just be wanted not because I am a girl or because I am a boy but because you are ready to lovingly embrace any child that is born to you. Otherwise, I will act like the opposite sex to please you. It scares me to death, quite literally, to feel rejected.

- <u>parents who take responsibility for their own happiness.</u> It should not be my burden to be responsible for that.

- <u>to be me not who you need me to be.</u> I want parents that will help me identify my areas of strength and help me cultivate them.

- <u>parents who, if I am a girl know better than suggest to me as a young lady that I won't be considered attractive nor lovable by any guy unless I'm skinny.</u> Rather, explain to me that some men, cannot with ease, make love to an average or large sized woman because their genitalia, when stimulated, won't enlarge enough to connect adequately. Don't let me make their anatomy my problem. That way I won't as likely become Bulimic. (Talk to me in straight forward manner kind of like "Auntie Mame".)

- <u>parents who eat healthfully and prepare healthful meals for me.</u> If you eat in unhealthy ways, I will come to believe that is the way we are supposed to eat. Your manner of eating will become a model for me to follow. Don't reward me with sweets or bribe me with an ice cream cone or soothe me with a doughnut. I will mismanage my emotions with food just as you would have taught me to do. And then, when I grow up and look fat like you, my only excuse for being obese will be, it's in the genes. No, it's in the thinking of the parent that I become the carbon copy. I am absorbing their negative self concepts and beliefs that then become entrenched as a debilitating habit.

- <u>parents who are relaxed with themselves and don't drive themselves to be the model 'perfect' parent, just a darned good one.</u> That will relieve all of us of the stress of having to be perfect for each other. I don't want to live life pressuring myself to be something it is not human to be consistently. I would rather be encouraged to excellence. There is a difference.

- <u>parents who are gentle and kind yet strict with me.</u> "No" must mean no. I need to experience behavioral boundaries and learn <u>self</u>-discipline. Otherwise, I will look to others and/or substances to control what I feel needs controlling in my life.

- <u>parents who foster faith.</u> I don't want to be distanced from the comfort of my heavenly Parent's embrace. Feeling all alone is frightening. Being guided to recognize the feeling of God's grace and unconditional loving presence becomes the rock of my foundation.

- <u>parents who themselves exhibit the delicious adventure of learning and growing</u> and who nurture a love of learning within me, even if I may not be as smart as the next one. Learning can be made to be fun. Being a failure in school can breed my being a failure in life. A love of learning and learning successes will give me a sense of accomplishment and self assurance.

- <u>parents who are able to get past having been programmed to have endless numbers of children.</u> It is not the end of the world if I am an only child if that is all you can honestly handle with care, patience, fiscal responsibility, and time. Question your real motives. I don't want to feel owned, trapped in your needs to have company nor like

I'm the only one you can depend on to love you. Please, surmount your fears of loneliness, of being unlovable, or, being devastated if I die before you. Please do not have another baby just in case. That is a decision that only takes <u>your</u> fears into account. Instead, think about the loss of a child the way you might the loving loss of a parent, a sad loss yes, but not a debilitating one.

We must be citizens of the world, responsible to this our Eden. I don't want to feel like a possession whose responsibility it is to alleviate your fears. Also, please keep in mind that our planet is shrinking in it's ability to feed us all as well as provide us with it's loveliness. Our world is being gobbled up with houses and endless humanity. We need to have a keen sense of the environment, and, a dedicated appreciation for the quality of life not simply life itself. People cannot thrive in crowded, ugly, noisy, savaged environment. I don't want to feel like a skittering rat freaked out by it all. In order for me to be at peace, it vastly helps to live in a serene environment. Now I realize no home, no state, no country is persistently serene. I don't need it to be especially if you are able to model the ways of constructive coping.

- <u>parents who are not drug, wrong food choice, nicotine or alcohol dependent.</u> I will learn from you the kinds of negative self concepts and beliefs that will cause me to be in some similar or same way dependent too.

- <u>the right to be nurtured by at least one of my parents full time</u> rather than being pawned off onto a grandparent, a part or full time nanny, occasional baby sitting or other daycare situation. These resources are for emergency situations.

- <u>a secure home.</u> Rough predicaments such as a father's loss of health or his loss of job happen. Are there savings to provide for us all while the rough time is weathered? Life deals curve balls. Hurricanes, for example, happen. Have you anticipated that fact and prepared for the contingencies **before** becoming pregnant? Your abandonment of my needs in order to serve your own needs doesn't seem fair. Having lots of babies in today's world is irresponsible. Worse yet, having lots of babies you can not really afford invites being on welfare. It does not do much for my sense of self nor does it teach me independence and self reliance. I don't want to come from a family structuring their lives to live off the largesse of others.

- <u>to be raised in loving not savage ways</u>. Calling me bad names helps me to become those bad names. Beating me encourages me to believe that is how I deserve to be treated. Also, beating me can create the belief within me that when I become a parent, I should treat my children for misconduct the same way. Violence is perpetuated in this manner. Moreover, when you beat me, and I come to believe that I must deserve to be abused or that I am too dumb to be corrected in any other way, I may marry someone who will treat me the same as you did.

- <u>parents who won't do everything for me but will teach me how to do for myself.</u>

- <u>parents who won't control my every waking moment nor belittle me when I have ideas of my own.</u> I must learn how to be independent or I'll freak out with the fear I don't know how. Help me to learn how to think for myself and how to solve problems. I must have critical thinking skills.

- <u>not to be your entwined companion.</u> Guide me to have trustworthy friends of my own.

- <u>parents who will talk and reason with me.</u>

- <u>parents who will play with me.</u>

- <u>parents who offer me genuine praise.</u>

- <u>to be raised in a home that is God centered.</u> I don't want an overblown sense of self importance nor a parent who is so full of him/herself.

Thank you for listening.

Addendum II

An Anatomy of Obesity

While the topic of obesity was alluded to earlier, I want to elaborate toward the goal of helping to reverse this terrible problem. As we know, this problem has attained epidemic proportion. It is a problem that produces much misery as well as health issues. Fat can become deadly. I refer to this problem as "death by fork". The death alluded to is not just death as in dying from heart disease, kidney failure or diabetes. It can produce the death of love, the death of joy, the death of mobility, the death of self respect.

Because you have read this book, you will be able to comprehend why diets generally work but only temporarily. Negative self concepts and beliefs, inexorably, will over-ride. They will return the unfamiliar lean self to the fat self. Moreover, the older a person becomes, the greater the number of lose weight gain weight episodes had, the more hopeless a person tends to become. Obese folks often 'throw in the towel' and that is when the real disaster begins. The fatter a person becomes the less mobile and the poorer the metabolic functioning. Muscle mass, which enhances metabolic functioning, dissolves the more immobilized a person becomes. Weight gain increases with less food required to do so. Fear increases, resulting in the increase of food consumption. Now, an obese individual feels hopelessly out of control.

For those with an obvious genetic component, research has to be done to find out just how much of a person's largeness is actually attributable to family genetic history. A woman's largeness attributable to genetics may be a size 14. Any size above that then can be attributable to negative self concepts and beliefs that lead to bad eating habits. The danger in blaming everything on genetics is that a size 14 woman will not have the ability, psychologically speaking, to be her 'normal' size. She will balloon beyond the 14 with the belief that her fat is beyond her control. After all, "it is in her genes".

Hypothyroidism, it seems, is generated to facilitate being large as well as to facilitate a person's self concept of being a depressed person. The subconscious, governed by the belief systems housed there, as you know, will effect a person's physiology.

Compounding the problem with obesity, is that physical education in our schools has been translated as competitive games and sports. Starting in preschool, age appropriate cardiovascular workouts and muscle development should be an essential part of the child's experience four days a week. Ballroom dancing would be a great physical education activity to offer starting around fifth grade. Games and sports should only be offered one day per week. In middle and high school, those who love sports can join Little League or other parent sponsored activities. The athletically gifted can be in sports activities taught at school.

After nineteen years of treating eating disorders here is a list of some of the 'ahas' uncovered.

- My Thanksgiving was ruined so, I'll enjoy feasting every day.

- Now that "my" children have been born, and, because I don't particularly care about sex, I'll get myself fat and unattractive to keep my husband uninterested. (Before getting pregnant, these woman are unaware, generally, of their strategy. Interestingly, during that time many of them actually do enjoy sex. They turn off just as many of their mothers' did, after childbearing.)

- I'll make sure I'll never get raped again. I'll get so fat no man will want nor be able to get near me.

- By being fat, it makes me invisible. When questioned under hypnosis why being fat would help her fulfill her self concept that she is supposed to be invisible she said, "people avert there eyes from you when you get really fat". "It makes them uncomfortable to witness your condition".

- I need some one to supervise my weight loss just like my mother did when I was a boy. This man's predicament had become an issue of 'other control'. He came to believe that he needed a female directing him to succeed with weight loss. Logically, as a female hypnotherapist, he came to me. My job, however was to free him not weigh him in. Moreover, my responsibility was to free him of the dependency belief and put him in charge of his own weight control program.

- I need to hide my genitalia. (When a man becomes severely obese, the folds of skin 'protects' him from exposure.) As a boy, this client was thrown out of the house naked by his angry father. Even though he pounded on the door and begged his father to let him in, his father was in no hurry to accommodate. As a boy, he was not just angry, he was enraged and ashamed of his genitalia. As an adult, his obesity served two purposes. One to keep him secure from being exposed. The other was a matter of vengeance. This client's grossness was specifically geared to make his father feel like a gross failure.

- By becoming fat, I won't be tempted to be sexy and seductive. That way I will be able to honor my marriage vows. This flirtatious yet very Catholic young woman found her solution to fidelity in obesity. Obviously, that negative reactive decision needed adjusting. So too did her beliefs around a need for provocativeness.

People have no clue as to their unique or not so unique 'aha' truth(s). Without this or some kind of exploratory process, they will remain victim to their ignorance. Direct suggestion hypnosis is not geared to exploration. When the subconscious is no longer bombarded with positive suggestions facilitative of weight loss, the weight gain will resume engineered by the negatives that are still there.

Generally speaking, the following are the typical decisions that generate obesity. The list includes: self/other punishment; absorbing someone else's pain; being other controlled; feeling unlovable; deserving of abandonment;

being taught to see oneself as fat; bad eating habits and concomitant beliefs learned in the home such as 'belonging to the clean plate club'; I am genetically predisposed to obesity; and, food is the only companion that I trust or want to give me comfort.

Self abandonment is probably the most common negative self concept that <u>hugely</u> contributes to the problem. It is a form of self disgust and self punishment. Moreover, as discussed earlier, encouraging a girl to be skinny (or not be lovable) is horrible. That is an absolutely terrifying idea for a teen to buy into. It creates a traumatic situation that generally leads to an eating disorder. The teen, when frightened in this or any other way, has access to her own subconscious mind and very likely she feeds it ideas that further traumatize her. Typical fears could include those of winding up all alone, believing she needs a man to take care of her, and/or she'll not be able to get married and have children, which will make her parents disappointed, plus the fear that she will be an ostracized spinster. <u>The fears multiply and become so bad</u> that binging feeds the fear frenzy, purging dumps the fears consequences. The individual has become quite literally, scared to death. When that person is ready to give up this binge with purge obsession, he/she needs to feel secure that obesity and feelings of being unlovable will not ensue. "Core healing" helps to ensue that outcome is less likely to occur.

One's self concepts and beliefs also need to provide the motivation for some one who adores food to change. We do not want to take away food's pleasure just the idea, for example, that more is better. <u>If we truly savor</u>

<u>food **less** is actually better.</u> Sitting down to a ten pound cut of Angus beef would nauseate most with the thought of having to eat it all in one sitting. There is a point of loss of pleasure. After a half of a pound? After one pound? Two?

If inflicting pain or absorbing a loved one's pain is the goal of obesity, then the person would consume as much as possible. Moreover, they would allow no pleasure awareness from eating such a delicious cut of beef.

Religious celebrations, celebrations in general, racial and cultural customs often make food central. Many foods associated with such customs are starch filled or sweet or fatty. Moreover, before we knew what was healthy eating as opposed to what was not, many became entrenched in unhealthy affinities. A cookie seemed better than a peach, white bread better than whole grain and more came to mean better. Less came to mean deprived.

How fat a person has chosen to become is also a critical issue. People do not realize that they have a target weight to help them actualize their subconscious purpose(s). Systematic neuro linguistic reprogramming has to occur to significantly improve the chances for amelioration of this epidemic.

978-0-595-37357-4
0-595-37357-7

Printed in the United States
49779LVS00005B/370-375